THE SOCIAL MESSAGE
OF THE
APOSTLE PAUL

THE SOCIAL MESSAGE
of
THE APOSTLE PAUL

The James Sprunt Lectures, 1942

By

Holmes Rolston, Th.D., D.D.

JOHN KNOX PRESS

RICHMOND   -:-   VIRGINIA

PRINTED IN THE UNITED STATES OF AMERICA

5586-(20)

TO MY MOTHER

JACQUELINE CAMPBELL ROLSTON

ONE OF THE PASSIONS OF HER LIFE
HAS BEEN TO SERVE HER GOD
THROUGH HER CHILDREN.
THIS BOOK IS DEDICATED TO HER
IN THE HOPE THAT
THROUGH ITS MINISTRY IN THE WORLD
THIS PURPOSE OF HERS
MAY IN SOME SMALL MEASURE
BE REALIZED.

The James Sprunt Lectures

This volume contains the Sprunt Lectures delivered at Union Theological Seminary in Virginia, February 1-7, 1942. Mr. James Sprunt, of Wilmington, North Carolina, in 1911 established a perpetual lectureship which would enable this institution to secure from time to time the services of distinguished ministers and authoritative scholars as special lecturers on subjects connected with various departments of Christian thought and Christian work. The lecturers are chosen by the faculty of the Seminary and a committee of the board of trustees, and the lectures are published after their delivery in accordance with a contract between the lecturer and these representatives of the institution.

As a result of this lectureship there have appeared twenty-eight volumes by European and American scholars. Among the former are such books as *Christian Psychology* by James Stalker, *The Mystery of Preaching* by James Black, *The Christian Apprehension of God* by Hugh Ross Mackintosh, *Conversion* by W. P. Paterson, and *The Church of Christ and the Problems of the Day* by Karl Heim; and among the latter are included such books as *The Religion of Power* by Harris E. Kirk, *Being a Preacher* by James I. Vance, *Fundamental Christianity* by Francis L. Patton, *Creative Controversies in Christianity* by George W. Richards, *A Preface to Christian Theology* by John A. Mackay, and many others.

More recently, in order to encourage the new generation of preachers and thinkers, the faculty and trustees decided to elect to this lectureship a certain number of younger scholars who had demonstrated capacity for productive thinking. The first of these was the Rev. Holmes Rolston, who had already shown the quality of his mind in the volume, *A Conservative Looks to Barth and Brunner*. The expectations of the faculty and trustees were not disappointed. Seldom has a series, on its delivery, been received with such enthusiasm. The reader will readily see why this was true. Dr. Rolston has with patience, insight, and freshness presented the social message of Paul. Some of his findings are familiar to New Testament readers and scholars, but the approach and conclusions are such as to make this volume a real contribution to the understanding of Paul's general positions on the social message and his dealings with specific problems. Here is a treatment of a subject which must engage the thinking of every Christian in these days of emergency and change.

B. R. LACY, JR.
President

Union Theological Seminary
in Virginia.

Acknowledgments

All quotations of the Bible in this manuscript are taken from the American Standard Edition of the Revised Bible and are used by permission of the owners of the copyright, The International Council of Religious Education. All italics in quotations of Scripture are mine.

I wish to thank the following publishers for permission to quote from books of which they are the owners of the copyright.

The Macmillan Company:

The Social Teaching of the Christian Churches, by Ernst Troeltsch.

The Divine Imperative, by Emil Brunner.

St. Paul's Epistle to the Ephesians, by J. Armitage Robinson.

St. Paul's Epistles to the Colossians and to Philemon, by J. B. Lightfoot.

Charles Scribner's Sons:

The Theology of Crisis, by Emil Brunner.

The Doctrine of the Word of God, by Karl Barth.

The Church and the Political Problem of Our Day, by Karl Barth.

The International Critical Commentary on Romans, by Sanday and Headlam.

The International Critical Commentary on Thessalonians, by Frame.

The Pilgrim Press:

The Word of God and the Word of Man, by Karl Barth.

The Round Table Press:

The Christian Message for the World Today, by E. Stanley Jones and others.

Wm. B. Eerdmans Publishing Company:

The Church and the Churches, by Karl Barth.

The International Missionary Council:

The World Mission of the Church—Findings of the Madras Conference.

Sheed and Ward:

Christianity and Class War, by Nicholas Berdyaev.

Random House, Inc.:

The Brothers Karamazov, by Dostoyevsky.

The Friendship Press:

Through Tragedy to Triumph, by Basil Mathews.

The Federal Council of the Churches of Christ in America:

A quotation from *The Federal Council Bulletin.*

Fortune:

A quotation from the issue for January, 1940.

———————

Quotations are made in this book from four books published in Great Britain and not copyrighted by an American publisher. They are: *Commentary on First Corinthians* by H. L. Goudge, and the *Commentary on Second Corinthians* by H. L. Goudge. These books are published in *The Westminster Commentaries* by

Methuen & Co., Sussex, England. They are retailed in the United States by Morehouse-Gorham Co.

The Fate of Man in the Modern World by Nicholas Berdyaev, published in *The Religion and Life Series* by The Student Christian Movement Press, London.

Theological Existence Today by Karl Barth, published by Hodder & Stoughton, London.

While permission is not legally required in the case of books not copyrighted in the United States, I have written these publishers, sending them copies of the quotations made and requesting permission to use them. At date of publication written permission has been received from Hodder & Stoughton and from The Student Christian Movement Press.

Every effort has been made to ascertain true ownership of copyrights and to give credit wherever due. If in any case this has not been done, proper acknowledgment will be made in future editions when fuller information is received.

I wish to thank Dr. Fitzgerald Flournoy, Professor of English at Washington and Lee University, for his criticisms of the literary form of the book, and Dr. J. J. Murray, Dr. J. C. Siler, Dr. Herbert Turner, and the Rev. Dunbar Ogden for their criticisms of the theological content of the book.

I wish to express my appreciation to Mr. John W. Hill, Manager of the Presbyterian Bookstore, Richmond, Virginia, for his evaluation of the manuscript from the point of view of the publisher.

And I wish publicly to acknowledge the splendid work done by Miss Zelda Lichliter, of Strasburg, Virginia, in preparing the manuscript for publication.

HOLMES ROLSTON.

Preface

This book is written in the conviction that the social message of the Apostle Paul has been unduly neglected in the thinking of the Christian church. Those who have gone to the Bible for its social message have centered their attention on the prophets of the Old Testament and on the teachings of Jesus. We would not in any way underestimate the great importance of these sources of the social message of the church, but over against them we can give at least two reasons for the peculiar relevance of the social message of Paul. In the first place, Paul writes against the background of a completed revelation. When Paul wrote, the great movement that began with Abraham and ended with the return of Jesus Christ to the Father was finished. Paul could view in its totality "the faith which was once for all delivered unto the saints." Paul was able to understand the meaning of human life as he stood in the full light of the revelation that came through Jesus Christ. This gives to Paul a point of view that was not fully shared by his predecessors.

In the second place, Paul writes to a Christian church in the midst of a pagan society. In the letters of Paul we have our earliest record of that process in which the church under the leadership of the apostles sought to adjust herself to the world in which she lived. It is our conviction that Paul was the leader who actually determined the lines along which the church adjusted herself to the society of the ancient world. But regardless of whether Paul directed this process or merely recorded it in his letters, it is to the writings of Paul that we must go as the major source of our knowledge of the way in which the New Testament church adjusted herself to the life of the world about her.

Paul's social message flows from his understanding of the meaning of the Christian faith. Paul spoke to the needs and problems of his own age. But he spoke as one who had stood in the light of the knowledge of the glory of God as he had seen it in the face of Jesus Christ. This book is an endeavor to catch Paul's point of view, to think Paul's thoughts after him, and to relate his message to the actual problems believers must face as they seek to realize the meaning of the Christian life in the midst of the terrifying world of the twentieth century.

Table of Contents

CHAPTER I

The Church in the Social Struggle

✦ ✦

IN THE introductory chapter of his book, *The Social Teaching of the Christian Churches,* Troeltsch says: "First of all, however, we must direct our attention to the Gospel, and to the Bible itself, and to the Early Church, for they constitute the permanent basis of our inquiry."[1]

The implication of Troeltsch's statement is obvious. Through the ages the church in her various branches has taught many contradictory things concerning the life of man in society. She has endorsed a married priesthood and she has forbidden her priests to marry. She has approved of monasticism and she has rejected it. She has supported slavery and she has pronounced the owning of slaves incompatible with a Christian way of life.

But throughout the whole of her life, the church has felt the inner necessity of showing that her social message flowed from the Bible. Of course this loyalty to the Bible has often been mere lip service. If there is one thing that Troeltsch's history of the social teachings of the Christian churches proves, it is that through the ages the church has derived a large part of her social

---

[1] From: *The Social Teaching of the Christian Churches,* by Ernst Troeltsch, Volume I, page 34. By permission of The Macmillan Company, publishers.

message from the prevailing culture of her social environment. If ever there was a process of reading into Scripture what was not there, it is to be found in the attempt of men to prove from Scripture social teachings that were derived from a source quite foreign to Scripture. As an example of this process, we might mention in our own generation the attempt to identify the evolutionary hypothesis of a social order that was to grow better and better and was gradually to develop into the kingdom of God with the radically different eschatology of the New Testament. But while the church has consistently drawn a large part of her social message from her environment, she has seldom, if ever, dared to confess that her social message has no vital relation with the sources of her life. If there has been a chasm between the social message of the church and the message of the New Testament, the church has always sought to hide it. She has never been willing to confess, boldly and without equivocation, that her social message did not flow from a true understanding of the word of God that was spoken through Jesus Christ.

It has remained for Karl Barth in his *The Doctrine of the Word of God* to give classic statement to the dependence of the church on the Bible as the source of her message. Barth works out his idea for the message of the church as a whole without any primary emphasis on the social teaching of the church. But the principles that he lays down for the message of the church as a whole are equally binding in the determination of the content of the social message of the church. Indeed, it is in this portion of her message that the church always faces her bitterest conflicts with the culture that surrounds her.

Barth writes: "For instance, as regards content, the Church's proclamation may not allow a question as to whether it is in treaty with the peculiarities and interests of a race, people, nation, or state. It cannot permit a question as to its agreement with the demands of this or that scientific or aesthetic culture of the moment. It cannot permit a question as to whether it is making the necessary contribution towards the preservation or perhaps even to the overthrow of this or that form of society or economy. A proclamation which takes up responsibilities in these or similar directions spells treachery to the Church and to Christ Himself. It only gets its due if sooner or later its mouth is stopped by some sort of delicate or brutal godlessness. Far better none at all than proclamation like that. Just because of its real responsibility, Church proclamation must be unconditionally free in every other direction. Its real responsibility arises out of its intention to be proclamation of the Word of God." [2]

Barth continues: "How disastrously the Church must misunderstand herself if, on whatever pretext, she can dream of being able to undertake and carry out anything serious in the certainly important fields of public worship reform, or social work, or Christian education, or the regulation of her relationship to State and society, or an international understanding among the Churches, without the necessary and possible being done simul-

---

[2] From: *The Doctrine of the Word of God,* by Karl Barth, page 80. By permission of Charles Scribner's Sons, publishers.

taneously in regard to the visible center of her life. As if it were patent on the face of it, as if we could confidently count upon it, that *evangelium recte docetur et recte administrantur sacramenta!* As if we could confidently leave that to God and meantime busy ourselves with the circumference of the Church's circle, which has perhaps been revolving for ever so long round a wrong center! As if we could actually put ourselves in God's hands without a single care as to what happens at this decisive point.

"Once more, how disastrously the Church must understand herself if she can imagine that theological reflection is a matter for quiet situations and times which suit and invite contemplation, a sort of peace-time luxury, to have no time for which is not only permitted but commanded, should circumstances become really serious and exciting! As if there could actually be, particularly for a Church attacked even externally, a more exciting task than that of making a beginning at proper inward consolidation, which means of course assiduous work at theology!" [3]

The church is today threatened with deadly attacks by such systems as Fascism and Communism. But it is not the task of the church in the presence of such attacks to see what she can do to adjust her message so as not to come into conflict with these systems. The church in the presence of such an attack must not be willing to seek to find her message in a source that is foreign to her life. The most that such an attack can do is to cause

---

[3] From: *The Doctrine of the Word of God,* by Karl Barth, page 85. By permission of Charles Scribner's Sons, publishers.

the church to go back to her records with a new concern to see if she has read aright the message that is contained for her in her Bible.

We state the same principle in a slightly different way when we say that reform in the message of the church must always flow from a new encounter of the church with her Lord. We are to study in this book the message of the church in some of the most critical issues of our time. We are to see the church in deadly conflict with the pride of wealth, or with racial hatreds and class distinctions. We are to dream of a church that seeks to build in our world a universal church which shall be a redemptive community in the chaos of modern international life. It is utterly vital that in such a study we shall not allow the pressure of the social struggle to cause us to seek to foster in the church a spirit that is foreign to her. Social reform in the church must not come merely because the church is trying to trim her sails as she is confronted with Communism, or Fascism, or Socialism. Social reform within the church must come because in the presence of these threats to her life the church has gone back to her Lord for a new understanding of his will for society.

The church must fear God more than she fears man. She must enter upon her reforms because in the hour of her need she has understood more adequately the meaning of the word of God to her in Jesus Christ. To those who fear that this may mean compromise and a dodging of the social issue, we venture to suggest that the demands of Christ on his church as he speaks to her through the New Testament may prove far more radical even than the demands of some theory of the nature of society. A true understanding of the demands of Christ on the Christian conscience in the midst of the race situation in the South may prove far more radical than the demands that would be made by some voice that came from a source that was foreign to the life of the church. A true understanding of the Christian doctrine of the stewardship of wealth may involve a dealing with money that is more radical than the demands of Socialism. The church will never be fearless in the presence of her adversaries unless she has learned first to fear her Lord more than she fears the face of man.

When the church finds herself within a cultural environment that is more or less hostile to her, her first task is to insist on her right to remain a church, i.e. on her right to seek to realize within her corporate life a fellowship that is based upon her understanding of the will of God for her. The church in Germany did not in the beginning come into conflict with National Socialism on the basis of an attack by the church on National Socialism as a form of government. The church was in the beginning quite willing to give National Socialism a chance to prove itself to be a *just* government. All that the church said was that within the National Socialist state, as in any other state, the church must have the right to order her own affairs in obedience to her Lord. It was in this spirit that Barth could write: "Speaking generally, the Church has not to be at the service of mankind, and so, not of the German people. The German Evangelical Church is the Church with reference to the German people: she is only in service to the

Word of God. It is God's will and work, if by means of His Word mankind, and of course, the German people, are ministered unto. . . . The Church believes in the Divine institution of the State as the guardian and administrator of public law and order. But she does not believe in any State, therefore not even in the German one, and therefore not even in the form of the National Socialistic State. The Church preaches the Gospel in all the kingdoms of this world. *She preaches it also in the Third Reich, but not under it, nor in its spirit."* [4]

The claim of the church to freedom within the state is not made, as in liberalism, on the right of every man to think as he pleases. The church merely insists that she must be free from every other form of social control in order that she may be free to be entirely under her Lord.

But the claim of the church to be free to develop her own life in harmony with the demands of her Lord is certain in time to bring the church into struggle with the social order. A culture that is not Christian cannot tolerate within its midst a fellowship that by its very existence calls in question the whole basis upon which that culture rests. This means persecution for the church, but it is persecution on the basis of the claim of the church to be a church. When reform within the church flows from Christ then the church can reply to the state that she must obey God rather than man. It is only as the church can say that obedience to the state means disobedience to Christ that the church will be

---

[4] From: *Theological Existence Today,* by Karl Barth, page 52. Hodder & Stoughton, 1933.

able to resist the attempt of the state to dominate her.

Whenever a group within the church comes into a new understanding of the will of God for the life of the church, there arises first of all a struggle within the church. There are certain to be divisions within the church. There will be groups that do not agree as to the will of God for the church today. There will be groups that differ in their understanding of the meaning for the church in her situation today of the word of God that was spoken in the past.

Whenever a prophet arises within the church to call the church on the basis of a new understanding of the demands of her Lord to the realization of a new life, there is certain to be division within the church. The prophet will find immediately that he is confronted by those within the church who have identified the will of God for the church with the compromises that the church has made with the social order in which she has lived. This means that in every advance of the church the first struggle will always be within the church. Often it is here that the struggle will be most intense. There will always be those who defend the compromises of the church as the true voice of God to the church. And the weight of custom and prestige is certain to be on the side of those who defend the compromises.

We find in the experience of Paul an illustration of the principle that in the beginning of a new advance within Christianity the first struggle will be within the church. Paul was called by Jesus Christ to open the doors of the church to the Gentiles. Because he was obedient to the heavenly vision Paul proclaimed that

the Gentiles were to be received into the church on
equal terms with the Jews. He proclaimed that both
Gentiles and Jews were saved by faith and by faith
alone. And in the beginning, Paul's opposition was
within the church. It was the Christian Jews who went
to Antioch and told Paul's converts that unless they
were willing to receive circumcision and keep the law
of Moses they could not be saved.[5] The Epistle to the
Galatians is directed against members of the church
who have come into Galatia to teach Paul's converts
that salvation was to be found through the law. And
it was not until Paul's fight had been won within the
church that Judaism became aroused to her danger. But
once aroused the Jews persecuted Paul with every means
at their disposal because they knew that the message of
Paul was a threat to the very existence of Judaism.

It is not by accident that we have in Germany today
a struggle in which the Confessional churches were
forced to draw out from the main body of German
Christians. It is in harmony with the same principle
that the issue of worship at the shrines has caused bitter
divisions within the church in Japan and Korea.

Of course we must not always assume that the
prophet is right and that those who oppose him are
always defending the sinful compromises of the church
with the social order. The church is at times faced by
false prophets who in the name of Christ would lead
the church to be disloyal to the true sources of her life.
The church in each generation must distinguish be-

---

[5] Acts, chapter 15.

tween the call of the true prophet and the call of heresy. But the general position is clear. Each new advance in the life of the church will first have to be fought out within the fellowship of the church.

The attitude of the cultural environment to the church is equally clear. As long as the prevailing culture can control the witness of the church it has no need to persecute the church. If the church in the Japanese Empire is willing to go to the shrines and to support the New Order in Asia, the Japanese government will not be forced to face the unpleasant task of persecuting the church. If the church in Germany is willing to come to terms with the German Christian movement, persecution can be avoided. If the church in Italy is willing to put her blessing on the destruction of the freedom of the Spanish people, and to throttle her witness in the presence of the cruelty of Fascism, the church can abide without serious conflict with the prevailing culture of Italy. If the church in the South is willing to attune its witness so as not to come into conflict with the demands of the ruling classes, the church can live at peace with the social order.

In fact, the culture within which the church moves would always prefer not to come into conflict with the church. Always, in one way or another, there is exerted upon the church the pressure of those who would control the voice of the church for their own purposes. The culture with which the church is at war always prefers to make a league with the church. When such a league has been made the clear cleavage between the prevailing customs of society and the will of God for His church does not at once become fully apparent. And in many cases the identification of the church with the culture in which it lives may be so complete that the church becomes one of the bulwarks for the support of the existing social order. Those who control the social order always prefer such a league, if possible, because through it they gain the appearance of the support of the Christian faith for their view of society. For this reason there is always a certain amount of pressure put on the church in the effort to throttle those things in her witness that might bring her into conflict with the dominating social group.

Because the great temptation of the church is the temptation to harmonize her witness to the demands of the social order, the church needs to hear constantly words such as those of Karl Barth to the German church as she was tempted to compromise her witness so as not to come in conflict with the demands of the Nazi party.

Barth writes, "What I have to say to all this is simply said. I say, absolutely and without reserve, NO! to both the spirit and the letter of this doctrine. I maintain that this teaching is alien, with no right, in the Evangelical Church. I maintain that the end of that Church will have come if this teaching ever comes to have sole sway within her borders, as the 'German Christians' intend that it shall. I maintain that the Evangelical Church ought rather to elect to be thinned down till it become a tiny group and go into the catacombs than make a compact, even covertly, with this doctrine." [6]

---

[6] From: *Theological Existence Today,* by Karl Barth, page 50. Hodder & Stoughton, London, publishers.

The church in other sections of the world does not face exactly the same issue that Barth faced in Germany. But the church does face similar temptations to compromise her witness. Until the social order itself becomes Christian, the church will constantly be faced with the temptation to speak softly just at those places where she should speak most fearlessly. And if the church is to discharge her function in society today she must be willing to refuse to compromise even when she knows that such refusals will mean persecution by the social order.

When the church permits her message to be identified with the presuppositions of a dominating culture, the church avoids persecution by that culture. On the other hand, the church, by identifying herself with a given culture, throws herself open to attacks by those who would destroy that culture. An obvious illustration in our time of a church attacked by those who would destroy the social order is to be found in the experience of the church in Russia. The Greek Catholic Church in Russia identified herself with the regime of the Czar. The church lived in the midst of an oppressed and exploited people. And the church as a whole did not permit herself to come into vital conflict with the unrighteous social order within which she lived. The church had a large stake in the existing social regime. She supported a despotism that is known as one of the worst despotisms of history. The church became identified in men's minds with the tyranny under which they were forced to live. And when at last men arose to break that tyranny they felt inevitably that they must attack the church because the church in their thinking was one of the bulwarks of the social order that they were determined to destroy.

But while this process is clearly illustrated in the experience of the church in Russia it is a process that is going on in many other sections of the world. Because of her stake in the old social order, the Catholic church supported Franco and the Italian and German Fascists as they sought to put down the revolution of the workers in Spain. And in the thinking of the masses of the Spanish people today the church is associated with the social order which has enslaved them. In a similar way, the progress of Christian missions in many sections of the Orient has been retarded because the native people have associated Christianity with Western imperialism. And while it may be impossible to know just how rapidly an antagonism toward the church may be spreading among the proletariat, the share-croppers, and the dispossessed of America, we must face here the general principle that when the church identifies her message with the interests of the dominating group in a social order she always lays herself open to attack by those who are the enemies of this group.

But we must not oversimplify the problem of the church in the social order by saying that the church is always attacked by the enemies of the social order because of the false identification of the church with the demands of the social order. We wonder what the Communists would have done if instead of the corrupt Russian Church they had faced in imperial Russia a church that in the purity of her life and witness was similar to the persecuted church in the Roman Empire during the first century of her existence. While it is true that the church is often attacked because of her unholy compromises with the social order, it may also prove true that the message of the church is incompatible with the point of view from which an attack is being launched on the social order. We express a partial truth when we say that Communism persecutes the church because it does not understand the true church. Perhaps if Karl Marx had known the church of the New Testament instead of the church he did know, he would not have been so violent in his attack on the church.

But we also express a partial truth when we say that Communism persecutes the church because it does understand the church. If the conflict between Communism and Christianity were merely the expression of the conflict between Communism and a false expression of Christianity, then it would not be difficult for this conflict to be resolved. But the truth is that just as the message of the church should have come into conflict with the despotism of the Czars so also the message of the church will inevitably come into conflict with the presuppositions upon which the Communist state is founded. The great conflict that is being fought out between Communism and Christianity in our world is not over a false issue. A Communism that offers itself as a way of salvation for mankind has become a religion, a religion the message of which cannot be harmonized with the word that the church must speak if she is to remain loyal to Jesus Christ.

In a similar way, we may condemn the compromises

of the Lutheran Church with the old Prussian social order in Germany.[7] Perhaps if there had been a different kind of church in Germany in the days of Prussian domination, Germany might have been saved from the road that she is walking today. But we must not say that the opposition of the Nazi party to the church is to be explained by the compromises of the church with her environment. The conflict between the Nazi party and the church is based on a true understanding both of the spirit of National Socialism and of the message of Christianity.

The church that has compromised her witness may avoid persecution from the prevailing social order. One of the dangers of such a compromise is that through her identification of herself with the social order the church may have to meet the attacks of those who would destroy the existing social regime. But through her compromises, the church lays herself open to that which is to her far more serious than an attack either by the leaders of the social order or by those who would destroy that society. The church that has compromised her witness may be called upon to face the wrath of her Lord. Jesus Christ is still the Lord of history. It is still true that all power is committed to Him on earth as well as in heaven. We must not think that the church in Russia perished without His knowledge or because He was unable to save her. Jehovah permitted the armies of Chaldea to destroy Jerusalem that the name

---

[7] Troeltsch has given us a superb statement of the nature of these compromises on page 575, Volume II, of his *The Social Teaching of the Christian Churches*.

of Jehovah might be purged from its association with the sin of Judah. And Jesus Christ may permit the destruction of a church that has borne His name, that His name may be cleansed from these associations. Or even if the church is not destroyed as an earthly organization, He may find the church so disloyal to Him that it becomes necessary for Him to remove the light of His presence from the life of the church.

To the great church at Ephesus, Jesus says, "Remember therefore whence thou art fallen, and repent and do the first works; or else *I come to thee, and will move thy candlestick out of its place,* except thou repent." [8]

It is the danger of this judgment that Barth holds before the German church as she is tempted to falter in her witness to her Lord. "Along with the external oppression of the Church she can be summoned to consider that God is at liberty to take away the light of the Gospel, if we do not want to have it otherwise. Even as He once removed 'the candlestick' from the North African Church, which was as much the Church of St. Augustine as the German Church is that of Luther. It would then be a fruitless and a silly thing to fight, by means of the instruments of Church-politics, against the sign given us in maybe one last moment in which all that mattered would be to cry aloud unto God, in the presence of this certainly fearful signal, that He might not be altogether weary of His rule amidst the great disloyalty of modern German Christianity and 'Churchianity,' and that He might be disposed to make

[8] Revelation 2:5.

us more loyal to His Word, by means of His Word, than we and our fathers have been." [9]

The church of Jesus Christ is made up of imperfect men and women. Until she becomes the church triumphant she will always be marked by the frailty, by the weakness, and by the sin that are characteristic of all things human. As long as the church remains the church militant she will remain an imperfect church, a church whose life is characterized by sinful compromises. Jesus Christ has chosen to use such a church as the instrument of His purpose in the world. The church of the New Testament was not a perfect church, but she was a true body of Christ. The communities that Paul built did represent a living witness to Jesus Christ.

Only Jesus Christ can say just when a church has proved so deeply disloyal to Him that He is forced to remove the light of His presence from the life of the church. But at the heart of every church there should be a holy fear. This fear is the *concern* of the church lest she prove so unfaithful to her Lord that in the end she is rejected by Him as the medium of His purpose in the world. Before the church can be utterly fearless in her social environment, she must hear again the voice of her Lord as He says, "Be not afraid of them that kill the body, but are not able to kill the soul: but rather fear him who is able to destroy both soul and body in hell." [10] Where this fear is found in the heart of the church, she will not be afraid of what man can do unto her.

---

[9] From: *Theological Existence Today,* by Karl Barth, page 73. Hodder & Stoughton, London, publishers.
[10] Matthew 10:28.

CHAPTER II

The Social Implications of Paul's Eschatology

+ +

THE chapter on eschatology must be placed in the beginning of a study of Paul's social thought, because Paul's social message roots in his eschatology. This statement of the origin of Paul's social message will not go unchallenged. There are many thinkers who have felt that because of his eschatology Paul was devoid of an effective social message. They have realized that Paul lived in the immediate expectancy of the return of his Lord. And they have argued that the expectancy of the immediate return of Christ could not be combined with a social program. Because of the prevalence of this feeling, it becomes necessary to examine Paul's eschatology for its bearing on his social message.

Eschatos is the Greek word for last. And the term, eschatology, is usually used to describe the portion of her message in which the church defines her teaching concerning the last things, i.e. the return of Christ and the final judgment. If we used the word in this narrow sense, a study of Paul's eschatology would be confined to a consideration of Paul's teachings concerning the end of the world. But the eschatology of Paul is a much bigger subject than his doctrine of the things that are to come at the consummation of the age. In discussing the eschatology of Paul, we must take into consideration *his whole view of the unseen world that confronts and qualifies the whole of our earthly existence.*

The two subjects are not divided. Paul's doctrine of the end of the age flows out of his understanding of the world of God that is already in existence. In fact, the consummation of the age is to Paul little more than the disclosure of the resurrection world of God which has already been in part revealed through the presence on earth of the resurrection life of Christ. The beginning of Paul's life as a Christian can be traced to that moment on the Damascus road when for his earthbound eyes the veil that hides the unseen was lifted and there was given to Paul a vision of the risen Christ in His glory. This was *a small moment* in the life of Paul. But it was the *small moment* that was determinative of the whole of Paul's life as a Christian. From this time on, he knew that Jesus of Nazareth whom the Jews had crucified was alive and glorified. He knew that he had seen within time that which established for him the reality of the resurrection life of God. For this reason, Paul shares with all of the apostles the insight that the life of the created universe cannot be understood apart from its relation to the world of eternity. Paul is sure that the life of the Christian in society must constantly be determined by the relation of the Christian to the world that has come to us in Jesus Christ.

We must think of Paul's eschatology in terms of his total view of the world of God that confronts, penetrates, qualifies, and determines the whole of our earthly existence. But when we have given adequate statement to this larger definition of Paul's eschatology, it does become necessary for us to look at Paul's eschatology in the narrower meaning of the word and to examine the bearing on Paul's social message of his view of the end of the world. In harmony with the purpose of the chapter as a whole, it does not become our purpose to give an exhaustive discussion of the nature of Paul's eschatology.[1] We are concerned merely with the study of the bearing of Paul's eschatology on his social message. For this reason we will content ourselves with a brief statement of what is generally accepted to be the message of Paul concerning the last things, and will then proceed to examine the relation between his views here and his understanding of the life of the Christian in society.

In discussing the early Christian belief in the nearness of the return of Christ, Sanday and Headlam write, "There can hardly be any doubt that in the Apostolic age the prevailing belief was that the Second Coming of the Lord was an event to be expected in any case shortly and probably in the lifetime of many of those living; it is also probable that this belief was shared by the Apostles themselves."[2]

A careful study of Paul's letters will lead us to the conviction that Paul shared the attitude of watchful waiting for our Lord's return which was characteristic

---

[1] *The Pauline Eschatology*, by Geerhardus Vos, gives a discussion of Paul's whole eschatology.

[2] From: *The International Critical Commentary on Romans*, by Sanday and Headlam, page 379. By permission of Charles Scribner's Sons, publishers.

of the early church as a whole. He taught men to live in the immediate expectancy of the return of Christ. And he taught his converts to be prepared at any moment for the return of Christ. In his teaching here, Paul is not to be set off as different from the other writers of the New Testament. A similar note of expectant waiting is to be found in First and Second Peter, in the Epistle to the Hebrews, in the book of Revelation, and indeed in the teachings of our Lord as they are found in the first three Gospels. The New Testament does not date the return of Christ. In fact, it insists that the knowledge of this hour is one of the things that is known only to the Father in heaven.[3] But the writers of the New Testament do urge Christians so to live that at any moment of their existence they may be ready for the coming of Christ and the final judgment. This was the characteristic attitude of the early church. It is an attitude which still exists in many sections of the church today.

Paul believed that the world in which he lived was moving forward to a consummation. In its negative sense, the return of Christ involved for Paul a time of judgment. To him, the coming of the Lord was to be a time of wrath for those who were not prepared for His coming.[4] To the Christians, the coming of Christ was to be a time of deliverance from their period of tribulation. The Christians were told to look for the day of their deliverance. Paul felt that the created universe was moving toward an end, i.e. toward a consum-

---

[3] Matthew 24:36; Acts 1:7.
[4] II Thessalonians 1:6-9.

mation in which the present world order would be dissolved and the resurrection world of God would be disclosed. He would have been in perfect sympathy with the statement in II Peter in which the Christians are described as those who according to Christ's promise are looking for new heavens and a new earth wherein dwelleth righteousness.[5] But the new heavens and the new earth which are described here do not come until after the coming of the day of the Lord wherein "the heavens . . . shall be dissolved, and the elements shall melt with fervent heat." [6] Paul felt that the created universe was moving toward a crisis in which the present world order would be changed and the resurrection world of God would be fully disclosed. He was not a pessimist, but he did not expect any complete redemption on this side of the time line.

Does Paul's view of the consummation of the age cut the nerve of social endeavor? Paul's eschatology has often been misinterpreted. Men may become so absorbed in the discussion of eschatology that their energies are no longer directed to the practical affairs of life. Men may become so sure of the coming of Christ in the very near future that they neglect to made adequate provision for the days that lie ahead. And there are indications that during his lifetime Paul's eschatology was abused in this way. But the evidence of the New Testament is that Paul was in constant struggle with those who would pervert his teachings concerning the return of Christ. Both of his letters to the Thessalonians

---

[5] II Peter 3:13.
[6] II Peter 3:12.

are written to curb the extravagances that have appeared in Thessalonica as an outgrowth of his teaching. He had utterly no patience with those lazy individuals who used his teachings as an excuse for quitting work.[7] He had no sympathy with those who were always announcing that the day of the Lord was just at hand.[8] And if Paul were with us today he would probably be in open conflict with those who have lost their sense of balance and proportion in their dealing with the eschatology of the New Testament.

When it is freed of the extravagances that have been grafted upon it, the eschatology of Paul does not cut the nerve of social endeavor. When the eschatology of the New Testament is viewed in the light of the history of the church, there is certainly sufficient uncertainty as to the time of the return of Christ to prevent men from using this eschatology as an excuse for laziness or indifference or inadequate planning for the future.

And it is the eschatology of the New Testament that has given to the Western world a sense of direction and purpose in history. Apart from its contact with the faith of the Bible, history has no real significance. This is true of Greek thought. It is equally true of the thought of India, or of China, or of Japan. The coming of Christ has given history a center and therefore a beginning and a consummation. Apart from the Christian faith, history has usually been conceived of in terms of the recurrence of meaningless cycles. The eschatology of

---

[7] II Thessalonians 3:6-15.
[8] II Thessalonians 2:1-3.

the New Testament has given history its sense of direction.[9]

The eschatology of Paul has not cut the nerve of the social message of the church. Strangely enough, it is through their eschatology that the New Testament writers were saved from the identification of their message with a special program that might not have been suited at all to the needs of the modern world. In discussing the effect of the eschatology of the New Testament writers on their message, Sanday and Headlam say: "It has been pointed out very ably how much the elasticity and mobility of Christianity were preserved by the fact that the Apostles never realized that they were building up a Church which was to last through the ages. It became the fashion of a later age to ascribe to the Apostles a series of ordinances and constitutions. Any such theory is quite inconsistent with the real spirit of their time. They never wrote or legislated except so far as existing needs demanded. They founded such institutions as were clearly required by some immediate want, or were part of our Lord's teaching. But they never administered or planned with a view to the remote future. Their writings were occasional, suggested by some pressing difficulty; but they thus incidentally laid down great broad principles which became the guiding principles of the Church. The Church therefore is governed by case law, not by code law; by broad principles, not by minute regulations. It may seem a paradox, but yet it is profoundly true, that the

---

[9] Reinhold Niebuhr discusses this subject on page 24 of *The Nature and Destiny of Man*, Volume I.

Church is adapted to the needs of every age, just because the original preachings of Christianity never attempted to adapt it to the needs of any period but their
own." [10]

In the argument which we have just presented, we
have been seeking to show that Paul's view of the
course of history and of the final consummation of the
age does not undermine his social message. Very often,
however, the basic objection to Paul's eschatology is not
so much a criticism of his view of the end of the world
as it is a violent opposition to the larger aspects of his
eschatology in which Paul sees man as living in a world
that is confronted and qualified by the world of God.
This objection is leveled not merely at Paul but also at
the whole Christian tradition.

As an example of this kind of criticism, there is the
charge of the Communists that religion is an opiate to
the people. The Communists openly charge that the
priests have drugged the people with fantastic promises
of a future heaven in order to make them content with
the burdens of this present life. Many Communists feel
that all thought of another world must be banished
from the minds of men in order that the workers may
arise with a supreme concern to realize within this
world a new order of life. Such men feel that the social
problems are needlessly complicated when men seek to
solve them on the basis of religion. And even the old
social gospel moved largely on the plane of the hori-

---

[10] From: *The International Critical Commentary on Romans,* by Sanday
and Headlam, page 381. By permission of Charles Scribner's Sons, publishers.

zontal. It had very little sense of the vertical. It failed to understand the life of man as a life lived out in time and in the presence of eternity.

It is true that those who have heard and understood the announcement of the supremely new order of God that meets us in the resurrection life of Jesus Christ are apt to have a certain detachment in which they no longer have an absorbing interest in the orders of this present world. But it does not follow at all that this sense of detachment from the world will cut the nerve of social endeavor within the world. It may be true that those who are in the world but not of the world can best serve the world. Certainly there is nothing in the life of Paul to make us feel that his eschatology cannot be combined with a life of intense activity in which the service of God bears fruitage in the service of man.

In evaluating the social implications of Paul's eschatology, we need to realize that any system of thought that has no answer to the great questions of man's origin and destiny must in the long run prove hopelessly inadequate to the needs of man. Men must inevitably ask those elemental questions concerning their origin, their meaning, and their goal. In the flush of early enthusiasm, men may give their loyalty to systems that rule out of consideration everything that is not of this world. But inevitably men must in time demand from someone an answer that deals with the meaning of their existence. And they must come to know that this answer is not found within the time order unless this order is seen as qualified and penetrated by the eternal world of God.

But today men are beginning to realize that even the social orders cannot endure unless they are set in their relation to an order that is above them all. In the despair of the modern world, we have learned that the social problems cannot be solved by a message that moves merely on the plane of the horizontal. Far from rejecting a social message because of its eschatology, we know now that a social message not grounded in an eschatology has no relevance for the modern world.

According to Nicholas Berdyaev, man can never be saved and the social problems can never be solved when life is thought of as moving only in the horizontal.[11] But the most remarkable evidence of this feeling in the modern world comes not from a theologian but from the editors of *Fortune,* the magazine of big business in America. In the closing paragraphs of an article published in this magazine they say: "Industrialists are not, should not be, and certainly do not claim to be spiritual leaders. The best they can do is to adapt such spiritual truths as they have been taught, to the requirements of the arena of action. Their progress in this direction is inevitably slow. But it will vanish entirely unless the initial teaching is strong, convincing, related to the contemporary scene, and consequently effective. In this regard it is all-important to observe that *the solutions to material problems are not to be found within materialism.*[12] This is just as true as the fact that democracy is not merely a collection of political bodies. By no

---

[11] See page 50, *The Fate of Man in the Modern World,* for development of this idea.

[12] The italics are mine.

conceivable set of circumstances could materialism have produced the great 'solution' of the eighteenth century that we have come to know as the American system. The American system has its origin, on the one hand, in passionate religious sects who believed in the spiritual absolutes that today are lacking; and on the other hand in those rationalists of the Golden Age of the American colonies, for whom Reason was not merely mechanistic but divine. Similarly, by no conceivable set of circumstances will it be possible to solve by materialism the titanic problems, domestic and international, with which humanity is faced today. *The ultimate answers to the questions that humanity raises are not, and never have been, in the flesh.*[13]

"Therefore it may be safely predicted that if these matters are left in the hands of the laity, to be solved on basically materialistic grounds, a gradual devolution will set in, and civilization instead of going forward so breathlessly will seem to recede. Without spiritual leadership the maladjustments of our politico-economic system must inevitably increase; unemployment, lack of opportunity, maldistribution of wealth, and lack of confidence will symptomize a long retreat; collectivism will grow; and what remains to us of the Golden Age when we were able to *believe,* will be consumed in revolutions and wars. *For the solutions to these things do not lie within these things.*[14]

"Second, so long as the Church pretends, or assumes to preach, absolute values but actually preaches relative

---

[13] Italics mine.
[14] Italics mine.

and secondary values, it will merely hasten this process of disintegration. We are asked to turn to the Church for our enlightenment, but when we do so we find that the voice of the Church is not inspired. The voice of the Church today, we find, is the echo of our own voices. And the result of this experience, already manifest, is disillusionment. . . . This is not a disillusionment in the ability of men to win wars, or to make peace after wars. This is a profound and absolute spiritual disillusionment, arising from the fact that when we consult the Church we hear only what we ourselves have said. The effect of this experience upon the present generation has been profound. It is the effect of a vicious spiral, like the spiral that the economists talk about that leads into depressions. But in this spiral there is at stake, not merely prosperity, but civilization.

"There is only one way out of the spiral. The way out is the sound of a voice not our voice, but a voice coming from something not ourselves, in the existence of which we cannot disbelieve.[15] It is the earthly task of the pastors to hear this voice, to cause us to hear it, and to tell us what it says. If they cannot hear it, or if they fail to tell us, we, as laymen, are utterly lost. Without it we are no more capable of saving the world than we were capable of creating it in the first place." [16]

The editors of *Fortune* have expressed in their own way the thesis we are defending. A social message that moves on the plane of the horizontal alone is not ade-

---

[15] Italics mine.
[16] From: Editorial in *Fortune* for January, 1940, page 27. Used by permission.

quate for the needs of our world. Our social message must flow from our theology. The social teaching of the church must be grounded in an adequate eschatology. We must be able to see the social sphere as it is penetrated and determined by movements that originate in the "above."

A social message moves merely on the plane of the horizontal when all of its motivation falls within the sphere of our visible earthly existence. A social message is penetrated by the vertical when men are urged to perform their duties to each other on the basis of an appeal that roots in the world of God that confronts our earthly life. For example, if we say that a firm must tell the truth in its advertising because the business of the firm will be injured if the public finds out it has been deceived, we are moving purely on the plane of the horizontal. If we say that a firm must tell the truth in advertising because God is truth and God demands truth in us, we are moving on a plane in which the vertical is penetrating the horizontal.

From this point of view we can see that practically the whole of the social message of Paul roots in his eschatology. For the motivation of his moral precepts, Paul always goes back to the realm of God. He passes from the great doctrinal part of Romans to the chapters that are filled with practical advice by telling his readers not to be fashioned according to this world but to be transformed by the renewing of their minds that they may prove what is the good and acceptable and perfect will of God.[17]

---

[17] Romans 12:2.

He opens the practical part of Colossians by saying, "If ye then were raised together with Christ, seek the things that are above, where Christ is, seated on the right hand of God. Set your mind on the things that are above, not on the things that are upon the earth. For ye died, and your life is hid with Christ in God." [18] In the twelfth verse of the same chapter, he says, "Put on therefore, as God's elect, holy and beloved, a heart of compassion, kindness, lowliness, meekness, long-suffering, etc." [19] The verses we have quoted are important because they mark Paul's thought of the Christian as living in two worlds. The Christian must move in the life of earth. But the roots of the Christian's life are already in that other world that has come to us in Jesus Christ. The Christian is called upon to live in one world and to bear witness to the other world.

But the closeness of the relation between Paul's eschatology and his social thought can only be grasped by going through his writings and noticing the way in which his moral and social message is related to his sense of the reality of the world of God that meets us in Christ. In later chapters in the book, these ideas will be dealt with in detail as we study the message of Paul to the Christian in the midst of the orders of society. They are given here simply to show the way in which his social message roots in his eschatology.

Paul calls men to forgive each other because God in Christ has forgiven them.[20] He tries to bring together

[18] Colossians 3:1-3.
[19] Colossians 3:12.
[20] Ephesians 4:32.

the divided church at Philippi by holding before them the example of Christ as He humbled Himself and laid aside His divine prerogatives.[21] He handles the question of eating meat offered to idols by reminding each Christian of his responsibility to the Lord.[22] He calls men to flee from fornication because the body is the Lord's.[23] He calls his converts to purity of life by telling them that no fornicator or drunkard can enter into the kingdom of heaven.[24] He tells wives to be obedient to their husbands because the husband is the head of the house even as Christ is the head of the church.[25] He tells husbands to love their wives as Christ also loved His church.[26] He tells children to be obedient unto their parents in the Lord.[27] He faces the problem of race by reminding us that in Christ Jesus there cannot be Greek and Jew, barbarian and Scythian; but Christ is all in all.[28] He faces the great division between slaves and masters by boldly asserting that it is transcended in Christ.[29] He tells slaves to do their work in the fear of the Lord, looking unto the Lord for the reward.[30] He reminds slave owners that they will be held responsible to a Master in heaven.[31] He condemns covetousness be-

---

[21] Philippians 2:1-10.
[22] Romans 14.
[23] I Corinthians 6:18-20.
[24] Ephesians 5:5; I Corinthians 6:10.
[25] Ephesians 5:22, 23.
[26] Ephesians 5:25.
[27] Ephesians 6:1.
[28] Colossians 3:11.
[29] Galatians 3:28.
[30] Colossians 3:22, 23.
[31] Colossians 4:1.

cause it is idolatry, i.e. because the worship of money conflicts with men's loyalty to the Lord.[32] He tells the rich to use their riches so as to lay up in store for themselves a good foundation against the time to come, that they may lay hold on the life that is life indeed.[33] He urges men to be content with food and raiment because they have brought nothing into this world and it is very certain that they can carry nothing out.[34] He seeks to curb human pride by reminding men that they have nothing they did not receive.[35] He challenges men to fight the good fight of faith that at the coming of the Lord they may receive the crown of righteousness that fadeth not away.[36]

The mere enumeration of these injunctions shows the way in which Paul's social message is rooted in his belief in the resurrection world of God. *Apart from his conception of all life in time as qualified by the existence of eternity, Paul's social teachings would be merely a collection of moral maxims without any unifying principle and without any relation to a source of power through which men would be able to keep them.*

Paul himself is convinced that if men cease to believe in the existence of the spiritual world which meets us in the resurrection, they will inevitably degenerate into a life that is devoid of meaning or of moral purpose. He tells the Corinthians, "If the dead are not raised, let us

---

[32] Colossians 3:5.
[33] I Timothy 6:17-19.
[34] I Timothy 6:7, 8.
[35] I Corinthians 4:7.
[36] II Timothy 4:6-8.

eat and drink, for to-morrow we die." [37] And when he has brought to a triumphant conclusion his great argument for the resurrection, he says, "Wherefore, my beloved brethren, be ye stedfast, unmoveable, always abounding in the work of the Lord, forasmuch as ye know that your labor is not in vain in the Lord." [38] The implication of this sentence is that if the Corinthians had lost faith in the existence of the resurrection life they could not have been sure that their labor in the Lord would not end in vanity.

We should not underestimate the restraining power on human conduct of Paul's doctrine of judgment after death. Paul taught that "we must all be made manifest before the judgment-seat of Christ; that each one may receive the things done in the body, according to what he hath done, whether it be good or bad." [39] He was sure that "we shall all stand before the judgment-seat of God," and that "each one of us shall give account of himself to God." [40] The earthly life of man becomes filled with significance and meaning when men believe that they must stand before the judgment seat of Christ. The fear of punishment after death acts as a restraining power over the evil of men. And the early Christians found in the hope of winning eternal life a goal that was worth all the sacrifices involved in being loyal to Jesus Christ.

When Paul is afraid that Timothy will yield to the

---

[37] I Corinthians 15:29-32.
[38] I Corinthians 15:58.
[39] II Corinthians 5:10.
[40] Romans 14:12.

threat of persecution and deny his Lord, he says to him, "Be thou sober in all things, suffer hardship, do the work of an evangelist, fulfil thy ministry." [41] Then he goes on to hold before Timothy the picture of "the crown of righteousness, which the Lord, the righteous judge, shall give . . . to all them that have loved his appearing." [42] In so doing Paul has laid his hand on the appeal that was to render the early church invincible in the midst of persecution. This appeal runs like a mighty refrain through the book of Revelation as the writer of this book seeks to brace the church for the terrible persecutions ahead of her. "To him that overcometh, to him will I give to eat of the tree of life, that is in the Paradise of God." [43] "Fear thou not the things which thou art about to suffer. . . . He that overcometh shall not be hurt of the second death." [44] "He that overcometh shall . . . be arrayed in white garments; and I will in no wise blot his name out of the book of life, and I will confess his name before my Father, and before his angels." [45]

Paul called on men to be Christlike—to stand for righteousness in the midst of an evil and adulterous generation. He braced them for the inevitable struggle and for all the sacrifices they were to make by fixing their eyes on the inheritance, incorruptible and undefiled, that fadeth not away, reserved in heaven for them.

---

[41] II Timothy 4:5.
[42] II Timothy 4:8.
[43] Revelation 2:7.
[44] Revelation 2:10, 11.
[45] Revelation 3:5.

In so doing he laid the foundation for a society of believers that even the mighty power of Rome could not crush. The church today may be entering a period of struggle with the powers of the world that is similar to the time in which the early church resisted the power of the Roman Empire. As part of the preparation for this struggle, the church today needs to understand the way in which her life in this world is rooted in her faith in the world of God. A Christian social message that is not related to the Christian eschatology [46] will not be able to withstand the attacks that are being hurled upon the church today.

------

[46] There is some division of opinion as to whether it is proper to use the word, eschatology, with the broad meaning ascribed to it in the latter part of this chapter. But in any case this is merely a question of terminology. The fundamental thesis of this chapter is that the social problems cannot be solved apart from the relation of man to the unseen universe revealed in the Christian faith. The validity of this thesis is not seriously affected by the terminology employed to express it.

CHAPTER III

The Radical and the Conservative Principles in the Social Message of Paul

✦ ✦

For the purposes of our study, the most interesting portion of the introductory chapter of Troeltsch's *The Social Teachings of the Christian Churches* is his treatment of the teachings of Paul. And the most arresting part of this treatment is the way in which he reveals the conservative and the radical principles that are present in the social message of Paul. We will quote a number of selected passages in order to show his general position, and then develop our theme on the basis of our discussion of his position. Troeltsch writes:[1]

"The Pauline world church ... did not merely recognize the State as permitted by God, but prized it as an institution which at least cared for justice, order, and external morality. . . . The Empire wields the sword according to the will of God and by order of God. But together with the order of the State there is recognized that which is inevitably bound up with it, the whole order of Society: the distribution of property, divisions of class and rank, in fact, the whole social organization.

"It is only natural that the conservative attitude should be applied to the institution of the family, which is

---

[1] In quoting Troeltsch, I do not express approval of all the positions he takes in these passages.

assumed as the basis of the whole of this ordered life. Marriage is used as the figure of the most important leading idea of Paul, that of the union of Christ with His Church. The existing patriarchalism, with the predominance of the husband, is accepted as the natural order, and submission to it is demanded as an ethical duty, while at the same time the husband also is urged most strongly to preserve his purity before marriage, and monogamous fidelity as well as personal self-giving in love to the wife and child are expected of him. The wife and the child, like the slave, are regarded as equal to the husband and the freeman in the religious and moral realm, and this actually, even if not in the eyes of the law, deepens and spiritualizes the whole of family life.

"Thus for many centuries the conservative attitude of Christianity towards political and social life was decided by this doctrine of Paul. It is a most remarkable thing that the entirely revolutionary and radical principle of unlimited individualism and universalism should adopt such a thoroughly conservative attitude to social questions. In spite of this, however, it actually exercised a revolutionary influence. For the conservative attitude was not founded on love and esteem for the existing institutions, but upon a mixture of contempt, submission, and relative recognition. That is why, in spite of its submissiveness, Christianity did destroy the Roman State by alienating souls from its ideals, and it has a disintegrating effect upon all undiluted nationalism and upon every form of exclusively earthly authority. But because its individualism and its universalism proceed from the religious idea and are related to religious values, such a conservative attitude is thoroughly possible.

"The principle which Paulinism here lays down, on the threshold of the great development of the future, is the duty of the recognition and use of social phenomena as organizations and institutions—which did not come into existence without God's permission and which contain an element of good—mingled with a spirit of inner detachment and independence, since, after all, these things belong to a perishing world and are everywhere steeped in paganism. This, however, suggested a positive relationship which was capable of further development and which was increasingly produced by the Early Church.

"The socially conservative development of Christian thought which is proved as an established fact mainly by Paul's Epistles, and which then received a lasting authority through the inclusion of these letters in the Sacred Canon, contains at the same time in some degree, however, the radical elements of Christian thought. These radical elements are directed purely toward spiritual renewal, the development of religious personality, and the fellowship of such personalities among themselves; combined with these ideas, is an other-worldly goal of ethico-religious perfection, which finds in the organizations of this present world useful points of support; these are regarded as merely provisional arrangements which have to be endured, and from which the Christian holds himself inwardly aloof. Thus for a long time the conservative and the revolutionary elements in Christian thought were united to and conditioned by each other in a classic manner, which constituted the general Christian standard.

"At this point, therefore, on the very threshold of the whole historical development, it is necessary to raise this question: Does this combination of conservative and radical elements correspond to the inner essence of Christian thought, or is it an accidental element due to the personal attitude of Paul himself and to the needs of the most primitive churches? Is it an essential characteristic of all the Christian social doctrines which has developed out of the central thought of Christianity, and thus already from the very beginning casts a clear light on the developments of the future? May it be that the two forms of social influence which have just been indicated, which are apparently diametrically opposed to each other, are not after all two equally possible applications existing side by side, but that perhaps they really belong to each other and are united in the fundamental idea from which they sprang? This seems all the more probable when we remember that the love-communism of the small primitive Christian community did not interfere with the world in which it was set ... and that Pauline conservatism had no inward interest in the values and standards of the present world, but that it only endured and used them as ordained and permitted by God. Although both these tendencies may at times diverge very widely, they might still perhaps be united in an inward relationship, and form a united stream of development for the sake of the great ends to be realized.

"It is my belief that, without danger of a forced construction, we are right in saying that *the Pauline turn of thought in relation to social matters corresponds to the spirit and meaning of the Gospel,*[2] and that in this respect it presents the classical example of the union of fundamental ideas right down to the beginning of the modern era. A religious doctrine like that of Christian monotheism which takes religion out of the sphere of existing conditions and the existing order and turns it purely into an ethical religion of redemption, will possess and reveal the radicalism of an ethical and universal ideal in the face of all existing conditions. But, on the other hand, just because it is a religious faith which believes that the whole world and its order is being guided by God, in spite of devils and demons, just because it means submission to the will of God who predestinates and allows all kinds of human differences to exist, it can never be a principle of revolution. So far it will always have a conservative trait of adaptation and submission toward the existing social order and social institutions, the conditions of power and their variations.

"On the other hand, however, that spirit of Christian submission and adaptation to circumstances will always stop short at the borders of the values of the inner life, of the religious-ethical world of ideals, and of the ecclesiastical organization which supports these ideals. In actual fact it will exercise a very profound transforming influence, and will venture on the most search-

---

[2] Italics mine.

ing interference with the social order; it will do this sometimes by indifference to existing conditions, sometimes by submitting existing conditions to the only valid test, the test of its own ideals and of its transcendent values; thus without any deliberately revolutionary intent, it will succeed in destroying and breaking down evil institutions and in inaugurating new ones. Its monotheism and universalism, its belief in Redemption and its ethico-personal inwardness contain a radicalism and a striving after unity which will always either ignore all merely temporal conditions or set them aside, and beyond all national and other forms of unity it will press forward toward an ideal religious unity which will be spiritual, inward, and living." [3]

We have quoted at considerable length from this stimulating discussion by Troeltsch. In the passages which we have quoted, Troeltsch discerns that in Paul there are two seemingly contradictory principles at work. One is a radical principle by which Christianity calls in question all the orders of society. The other is a conservative principle by which Christianity recognizes the orders of society as orders of creations or as orders of history that have in part been willed of God. On the one side, we see Christianity moving as a revolutionary force in social life, a force that has been most effective in destroying those things in the social order which were not Christian. On the other hand, we see Christianity moving as a conservative force that recognizes

[3] The quotations are taken from pages 79-86, Volume I, of *The Social Teaching of the Christian Churches,* by Troeltsch. By permission of The Macmillan Company, publishers.

the orders of society and urges obedience to them as the will of God for society.

Troeltsch is right in clearly distinguishing this seeming paradox in the Christian social message. He is right also in tracing these principles back to Paul. He acknowledges that these principles have been in the Christian message through the ages because they were in Paul at the beginning. Troeltsch is right also in his understanding that "the Pauline turn of thought in relation to social matters corresponds to the spirit and meaning of the Gospel." We do not have here a system that is foreign to the message of Jesus. The Pauline thought corresponds to the inner meaning of the gospel. It represents a true understanding of the nature of the social message of the church. In fact, a knowledge of these principles is so essential to an understanding of the social message of Christianity that we can almost say that *he who has not grasped this inner dialectic of the Christian social message has not understood at all the movement of Christianity in the social order.*

Troeltsch has given us a superb statement of these seemingly contradictory principles, but he has failed to give an adequate statement of the basis in Christian thought in which these principles are grounded. He does not know (and on the basis of his understanding of Christianity he could not know) that Paul's revolutionary principle roots in his eschatology and that his conservative principle roots in his knowledge of human life as lived out in the midst of sin and judgment.

The basis in the thought of Paul out of which these principles flow will become clear as we examine the radical and the conservative tendencies in Paul as they are illustrated in some of his teachings. The two principles emerge clearly in his treatment of the relation of man and woman to each other. We know from Jesus that the whole principle of sex belongs to the life of earth, and that this order of creation is not perpetuated in the resurrection life of God. "And Jesus said unto them, The sons of this world marry, and are given in marriage: but they that are accounted worthy to attain to that world, and the resurrection from the dead, neither marry, nor are given in marriage: for neither can they die any more: for they are equal unto the angels; and are sons of God, beings sons of the resurrection." [4] The thought of Paul is in harmony with the position of Jesus. He boldly declares that in Christ Jesus there is neither male nor female.[5] Paul knew also that the church was called upon to build on earth a society whose corporate life witnessed to the life of that heaven in which the distinction of sex had dropped out. No one can measure the effect of this principle of Paul's on the emancipation of woman. It has presented woman as standing before God on an equality with man. It has demanded that there should be realized on earth a society in which every woman received her rights as an immortal soul with an eternal destiny.

But Paul recognizes also that the whole matter of sex is an order of creation. He knows that even as it was said that man was created in the image of God it was

---

[4] Luke 20:34-36.
[5] Galatians 3:28.

also said, "male and female created he them." [6] A Christian ethic must not forget that in the world of eternity the distinction of sex drops out. But a Christian social message that ignored the distinction of sex would break itself on the rock of reality.

Paul goes further than the recognition of the order of sex as an order of creation which is characteristic of all of our earthly life. He knows that our life in this present world is lived out in sin, and that within the realm of our sinful existence certain orders of life have developed that may in a limited sense be considered orders of history which are willed of God as necessary for our earthly life in its present state of development. Because of this, he who wrote that in Christ Jesus there is neither male or female but a new creation can also write, "Wives, be in subjection to your husbands, as is fitting in the Lord." [7]

The principles which we have illustrated as they are to be found in Paul's treatment of the relations of men and women are present in all of the social teaching of Paul. Consider in this connection Paul's treatment of the problem of slavery. Paul is aware of the end of all orders in the inexpressibly new order of the kingdom of God. He declares that in Christ Jesus there is neither bond nor free. He reminds the slaves that they are the Lord's freemen; the owners that they are the bondmen of Christ; [8] the masters that they have a Master in heaven. [9]

---

[6] Genesis 1:27.
[7] Colossians 3:18; Ephesians 5:22.
[8] I Corinthians 7:21, 22.
[9] Colossians 4:1.

In spite of these radical and far-reaching principles, the message of Paul to the institution of slavery is essentially conservative. He tells the slaves to be content to remain in their position of life.[10] When he finds that Onesimus is a runaway slave, he tells him that he must return to his master, and in his beautiful letter to Philemon he does not demand that Philemon should set Onesimus free.

In a similar manner, Paul wages the fight of his life over the power of Christianity to break down the barriers between Jew and Gentile. He declares that in Christ Jesus there is neither Jew nor Gentile. As he sets his face toward Jerusalem, he is ready to give his life in his attempt to hold together the Jewish and Gentile elements in the church.[11] But he tells the Gentiles not to become circumcised and the Jews to remain in circumcision.[12]

He honors the rulers and recognizes the state as ordained of God. But he builds in the Roman Empire a society which moves on a set of principles which are foreign to the Roman state. The acceptance of the state as ordained of God was so strong in Paul that his message here was easily perverted to a support of the doctrine of the divine right of kings.[13] But the society which Paul built owed its supreme allegiance to Jesus Christ, and because of this allegiance within a few years this society was to be involved in a life-and-death strug-

---

[10] I Corinthians 7:20, 21.
[11] Acts 20:24.
[12] I Corinthians 7:18.
[13] Consider in this connection Romans 13:1-7 and I Peter 2:13-17.

gle with emperor worship. And if kings have appealed to Paul for the support of their claims to rule by divine right, it is also true that the roots of democracy are to be found in such Pauline doctrines as the infinite worth of each individual—a worth that depends on man's eternal destiny and therefore on eschatology—and the equality of all men before a God who is no respecter of persons.

We have given a number of illustrations in order that through them we may reveal these two seemingly contradictory principles as they exist in the message of Paul. Paul proclaims the supremely new order of the world of God. He tells churches to build on earth a corporate life that bears witness to that other world in which their life is rooted. He writes to the Colossians, "If we then were raised together with Christ, seek the things that are above, where Christ is, seated on the right hand of God. Set your mind on the things that are above, not on the things that are upon the earth. . . . ye have put off the old man with his doings, and have put on the new man, that is being renewed unto knowledge after the image of him that created him: where there cannot be Greek and Jew, circumcision and uncircumcision, barbarian, Scythian, bondman, freeman; but Christ is all, and in all." [14] This is the radical message of Paul.

At the same time Paul does not assume a revolutionary attitude toward the orders of creation and history within which the life of the Christian in society must

[14] Colossians 3:1, 2, 9-11.

be lived. He does not deify these orders. But he does urge the Christian to accept them and to acknowledge that they represent the will of God in that they constitute the God-given social situation within which the Christian must live out his earthly life. In this sense, Paul's social message is a conservative force in the midst of society.

When we have stated the two principles that undergird the social message of Paul, we must go further and study them in their bearing on his message and in their relation to each other. Paul's radical principle in which all the lesser orders of life are judged by the supremely new order of the kingdom of God is balanced by his conservative principle in which the existing orders of society are tolerated as part of the God-given pattern within which the life of the individual is to be lived. And because of the balance of these two principles Paul is saved from the absurdity of *proclaiming an absolute ethic in the midst of a sinful world.*

All too often the Christian preacher has proclaimed a social message which is utterly impossible of realization in the actualities of the social situation within which the Christian is called upon to realize the meaning of a Christian life. To proclaim without compromise the demands of an absolute ethic in the midst of a situation in which this ethic cannot be realized may at times be both foolish and sinful. This has been the fatal weakness in all idealism. The program that is set for us by an idealistic ethic becomes impossible of application because such a program has usually ignored the actual conditions which form the framework within which the Christian must seek to know and to do the will of God for him.

We may illustrate this principle by considering its application to the problem of slavery in Paul's time. Paul knew that the social and economic distinction between bond and free was transcended in Christ. He knew that this belonged to an order of life that did not carry over to the kingdom of God. He told masters and slaves that they must realize in Christ a common brotherhood. But what would have happened if Paul had been uncompromising in the application of this principle? What would have been the consequences if Paul had told slave owners that as a condition of their reception into the fellowship of the church they would be required to emancipate their slaves? What would have happened if Paul had told the slaves of the Roman Empire that because slavery was not a Christian institution they would be justified in running away or in rising against their masters? What would have happened if such an interpretation of the meaning of Christianity had been made authoritative for the church in the Roman Empire of the first century?

Such an interpretation of the meaning of Christianity would have resulted in the identification of Christianity with a radical social movement that struck at the whole basis of the economic life of the Roman Empire. It is obvious also that because of such an identification the gospel which Paul preached would have lost its distinctive note as a message of personal salvation coming to the individual in the midst of his God-given situation in life.

We can illustrate the same principle by a glance at Paul's message concerning the bearing of the gospel he preached on the relations of men and women in the Roman society. Paul knew that in Christ Jesus there was neither male nor female. He boldly lays down the radical principle that was to be a ferment working in the world for the emancipation of woman from the domination of man. But what would have happened if Paul had sought to overturn in the name of Christ all of the existing customs in Roman society through which the ancient world had learned to regulate the relations of men and women? Such a move would have done more harm than good. The ancient world was not prepared for such freedom in the relation of the sexes. And even after centuries of Christian tradition Paul's radical principle of the equality of men and women must be applied with a degree of caution. Even if it is done away in heaven, the distinction of sex is a permanent feature of our earthly life, and all social institutions must be adjusted to this fact.

But while the radical principle in Paul must be balanced by his conservative principle, the observance of the conservative principle must never be allowed to choke the witness of the church in her corporate life to the world of God in which she is rooted. It may be necessary for Paul to send Onesimus back to Philemon. But neither Philemon nor Onesimus is to be permitted to forget that because they are both in Christ they are brothers. Paul may recognize the authority of the man in the home as an order of Roman society which the church must tolerate. But the husband must never be permitted to forget that he is living with one who is an heir with him of eternal life.

Paul recognizes the Roman state as ordained of God for the preservation of law and order. He commands the Christians to obey the magistrate not only because they are afraid of him but also for conscience' sake, as resistance to the magistrate is resistance to an ordinance of God.[15] But when the state ordered the Christians to worship the emperor the church that Paul founded was capable of saying that the worship of the emperor was a denial of the deity of Christ and that before Christians could yield here they must be ready to go to prison or to death.

The inner witness of the church must always be preserved. The church, it is true, must recognize and tolerate the existing orders of society. But there are many points at which the church cannot compromise. The relation between the radical and the conservative principles must always be that of tension. And the basic interest of the church must always be on the side of the radical principle. The church is supremely interested in the new order of God which she proclaims. She recognizes the existing orders of society. She knows that because they do exist they are in a limited sense a part of the God-given situation within which she must live. But the church is not primarily interested in the preserving of any of the existing orders. And because she does proclaim the kingdom of God the church is constantly in the midst of a process in which she ultimately

---

[15] Romans 13:1, 2, 4, 5.

destroys those things in her social background which she comes to understand as out of harmony with the purpose of God for the life of man.

Judged from this point of view, much of church history can be understood as a conflict within the church between the radical and the conservative tendencies that are inherent in the Christian faith. Through a misunderstanding of the dialectic nature of his social thought Paul has been quoted on both sides of almost every hotly contested social issue within the church.

A typical example of this is the struggle over slavery that went on within the church a few generations ago. After a long period of historical development there came at last to men the insight that the whole system of slavery was wrong. The reformers were right when they said that human beings with immortal souls were not chattel to be bought and sold in the market place as stock. The men who opposed slavery did so because they were Christians. In the name of Christ they declared that this institution must go. The radical principle in the Christian message had led the world to the demand for the abolition of slavery.

No one defends slavery today. No one has any reason for defending slavery now. It has been abolished long enough for the economic and social life of the world to have adjusted itself to a world in which slavery does not exist.[16] But the demand for the abolition of slavery met in the southern part of the United States a social culture and an economic procedure that were built

---

[16] This is not to say that our present order of society does not have institutions which may be as unchristian as slavery.

around slavery. In this situation, those who wished to defend slavery fell back on the conservative principle of Paul. They visualized slavery as an ordinance of God. They felt that the church was called upon to preserve slavery. They declared that the abolitionists were non-Christian. To those who wished to make the attitude toward slavery a test of church membership, they replied that Paul did not put Philemon out of the church because he owned slaves. They reminded the abolitionists that Paul sent back a runaway slave. Paul was on both sides of the struggle.

The real tragedy of the whole situation was that the conservative principle in Paul was being used to preserve an economic order whose time in history was past. Through their failure to understand the full message of Paul those whose economic interests were identified with the preservation of slavery were seeking to find in the message of Paul the support for the permanent perpetuation of an order of society that was essentially unchristian.

The tension between the radical and conservative principles in Paul is seen in the controversy that still goes on within the church for the equality of woman with man in the life of the church. Paul sets forth the great dynamic principle that in Christ Jesus there is neither male nor female. He tells his converts to build a life on earth that is a witness to the world of heaven. He knows that in the world of heaven the distinction of sex has dropped out and men and women stand before God on a position of complete equality. Because of these principles which are to be found in the thought

of Paul, Christianity has always been a ferment working for the emancipation of woman. No one can overestimate what Christianity, even in our generation, has
done for women in such non-Christian lands as China,
Korea, or Africa. Dr. Egbert W. Smith, the Educational Secretary of Foreign Missions for the Presbyterian
Church in the United States, tells in one of his addresses
of the way in which some branches of the church in
China have taken action placing woman within the
church there in a position of complete equality with
man. When you consider the place of woman in the life
of the old China, such an action on the part of the
Chinese church is a remarkable tribute to the power of
Christianity to work for the equality of woman.

But the conservative principle is also at work in the
writings of Paul. In the order of the home he places
woman in a subordinate position to man.[17] And he
gives woman a subordinate position in the life of the
church. The elders and deacons in his churches are
men. He tells the women to remain veiled in the
church.[18] He orders the women to "keep silence in the
churches." [19]

The tension between these two principles of Paul
still exists within the church. In many churches it is
not considered proper for a woman to speak in a con-
gregational meeting. Most churches elect only men to
the board of deacons or the board of elders. With the
emancipation of woman, most of the professions have

---

[17] Colossians 3:18; Ephesians 5:22.
[18] I Corinthians 11:13.
[19] I Corinthians 14:34, 35.

been opened to them. But most churches are not ready to ordain a woman to the ministry. The way in which woman still struggles against the conservative principle of Paul is illustrated by a clipping from the *Presbyterian of the South*. It is headed, "Last Stronghold of Male Dominance."

"Miss Georgia Harkness, who teaches philosophy at Mount Holyoke College,[20] is a minister of the Methodist Church, and one of our most gifted writers on religious themes. She called the church 'the last stronghold of male dominance' at a Methodist Leadership School this summer at Lake Junaluska. 'The fact that women frequently put their energies into channels which lie outside the church,' she said, 'is often deplored by men who have the interests of the church at heart. . . . These other agencies offer women an opportunity for leadership, for creative expression—and in turn a recognition which they do not find within the church. Until the men of the church recognize this fact, to deplore the defection of women will largely be wasted breath.' "

Over against this picture of the church as the last stronghold of male dominance, there can be set a paragraph of the report of the Madras Conference. This quotation is taken from the section that deals with Women's Work. "We recognize with gratification that women in a number of countries have rendered constructive service as ordained ministers, elders, deaconesses, members of Religious Communities, and lay

[20] Miss Harkness is now Professor of Theology at the Garrett Biblical Institute, Evanston, Illinois.

leaders. We believe that more women should be included in the membership of administrative and executive boards and councils of the Church. It is the conviction of many that ordination into full ministry of the Church on terms of equal status with men should be opened to women of mental ability, spiritual gifts and devotion to the call of Christ. . . . The unity of the Church can never be fully realized until all members of the Church—women as well as men—share more fully in its task." [21]

It would be tragic if Paul's authority were to be used to make permanent within the church the present status of woman and to prevent the church in obedience to her inner life (which also comes from Paul) from building on earth a fellowship in which the emancipation of woman from male dominance has become complete.

If we are to understand the social message of Paul at all, it is essential that we should understand the interaction between the radical and the conservative principles in his message. We will elaborate by considering them as illustrated in the work of the foreign missionary. When the missionary goes to a portion of the world that has not known the gospel, he is certain to face a society in which a pagan culture is deeply entrenched. He will have to work in a world in which the orders of society have been determined by non-Christian conceptions as to the meaning of human life.

---

[21] From: *The World Mission of the Church*—Findings and Recommendations of The International Missionary Council, page 149. Used by permission.

The message of the missionary in this situation will be first of all a message of individual redemption. The missionary will follow in the footsteps of Paul as he seeks to lead individual men and women to know the Christ whom to know aright is life eternal. But the missionary will soon be faced by the dilemma of Paul. His converts will be forced to continue their life in the midst of a pagan culture that has developed into definite orders of history centering around the family, the tribe, the nation, etc. The missionary will have to advise his converts concerning their life in this situation.

The task of the missionary will grow more complicated as the church grows. As the converted individuals are gathered into churches, the missionary will have to interpret to his converts the demands of Christ for the corporate life of these communities. As the various Christian communities seek to realize a wider Christian fellowship within the life of the nation, the missionary will be forced to try to define the relation of the church within the nation to the various orders of society around which the national life has been developed. As the national church seeks to take its place within the fellowship of a universal church, the missionary will be faced by situations in which it is increasingly difficult to define the content of the Christian message.

In the midst of this situation, the missionary of today will have at least one advantage over Paul. He will face his task with the light of many centuries of church history behind him. If the missionary has come from a country that has been evangelized for a long time, he will have the advantage of having seen the form which the orders of society have assumed as they have been modified by their contact with the Christian message.

But even with these advantages at his disposal, the Christian missionary of today must follow a method similar to that of Paul. There will be places where he will make very clear the meaning of the Christian message. The converts will not be permitted to engage in the idolatrous rites of heathen worship. The Christian ideal of monogamy will be held forth as the basis of family life. But the wise missionary will seek to make as little disturbance as possible in the outer form of the social order in which the infant church must operate. The probability is that the government of the country in which the missionary is at work will be a dictatorship which does not approximate very closely the Pauline conception of a just state. But even if he does not always approve of this government, the missionary will make it clear that he is the bearer of a message of individual redemption and that he is not entering the land to organize a revolution against the government of the country. The missionary will advise his converts to obey the law of the land in so far as such obedience does not conflict with a personal loyalty to Christ.

The missionary will not attempt to overturn all at once the ancient customs that are connected with marriage and the family life. These things must be penetrated from within before they can be wisely altered in their outer form. In the same way, the missionary cannot ignore all of the realities of the race situation. He will seek to build a fellowship that bridges race, but he will not want his children to intermarry with the members of another race until Christianity has been given time to create a common social culture in which the children of such marriages can find a background for a life that is not constantly filled with tragedy.

There are two mistakes that the missionary must not make. On the radical side, he must not identify the Christian message with a social revolution that will call in question all of the established forms of the society in which the church must live. On the conservative side, he must not preach a gospel of individual redemption that is so detached from life that it makes no impact on the unchristian elements of the social life of the nation. Between these two poles, the missionary must seek to interpret to his converts the meaning of the Christian message in the actual social situation in which these converts must live. In so doing he will live in the midst of the tension which is inevitable when we understand both the radical and the conservative principles that are at the heart of the Christian message.

Our consideration of the conflict in the church between the radical and the conservative tendencies in Paul leads us to another major insight into the nature of Paul's social message. As we seek to apply the social message of Paul to the situation in which we move *there must always be involved an element of historical decision.* Within large areas of our social life there is no absolutely clear-cut understanding as to the implications of the Christian message. Most of us would like to have an absolute ethic that freed us in all cases from the necessity of a decision as to the will of God for us in the historical situation in which we stand. We do not have such an ethic, and we can never have it as long as the Christian is called upon to bear witness to the resurrection life of God in the midst of a sinful society.

Within certain areas of life, the will of God for us is comparatively clear. No Christian is ever called upon to lie, or to steal, or to commit adultery in the service of God. But within that vast realm in which the Christian must work out his relation to the orders of the society in which he moves (and this is the realm which concerns us now) there is no absolutely binding social message which enables us to avoid the necessity for historical decision.

In every situation which the church faces she is called upon to decide what must be said in the here and the now on the basis of what has already been said in the there and the then. Her word to the present situation must be made on the basis of the word that was spoken to her in the time of her origin. But if her word to the present situation is to be a real word it must have in it an element of historical decision that is related to the concrete situation which the church faces. The church stands in the midst of a sinful society. She is called upon to bear witness to the world of God that meets us in Christ. In such a situation, the message of the church must flow from her understanding of the inner relation between the conservative and the radical principles that are her heritage from Paul. The word which the church speaks to the social situation must bear witness to Christ, and at the same time it must be a real word which comes from the understanding of the church as to that which is possible in the actual social situation in which she moves.

As we face this inevitable tension in the life of the church, we would be wrong to conclude that those who hold to the radical principles are always right. In some situations it would be sinful to seek to hold the church to an absolute ethic that had no relation to that which was possible in the actual historical conditions the church was facing.

We can illustrate this truth by a consideration of the whole idea of passive resistance as it has been developed by Gandhi. There is very much to be said for this type of resistance to tyranny. It involves suffering, but it involves suffering that is voluntarily assumed in a way that leads to the spiritual development of the one who suffers. In contrast to war, the method of Gandhi does not tend to engender hate. His method has proved particularly effective in the struggle of the people of India against oppression.

But the method of passive resistance depends for its effectiveness on the freedom to carry out a program designed to arouse public opinion and on the presence of an enlightened conscience in the nation or in the class group to which the appeal is being made. As a method of resisting the expansion of the power of National Socialism, a program of passive resistance might have meant the weakening of the power of the nation to resist until the way was prepared for the establishment of a tyranny within which the church could no longer function. The world has often suffered far more from the idealists than from the realists. And it is very probable that the lack of a realistic facing of the type of force by which Western civilization is threatened today is responsible for the collapse of freedom in the continent of Europe.

An illustration of the same principle can be found in the history of the United States. In spite of our love of freedom and our hatred of slavery, and in spite of our deep appreciation of the religious motives that lay behind it, we cannot but feel that the abolition movement must bear some measure of sinful responsibility for the War Between the States. The abolition movement had in it a passion for freedom. Its demands were rooted in an understanding of the meaning of the Christian message. But the abolition movement had no understanding of the concrete historical situation within the social order of the South. The violence of the abolition movement produced a reaction that prevented Christianity in the South from undermining the curse of slavery without the cost of a war that shook the American nation to its foundation—a war from which the South has never fully recovered. And the memories of the days of reconstruction have made it difficult for Christians in the South to think sanely on a subject that demands all the wisdom they have.

And while we are ready to acknowledge the exceeding sinfulness of Southern society in its perpetuation of racial injustice today, we do have a right to ask that the word which the church seeks to speak in this situation shall arise out of a knowledge of the actual conditions faced in the South.

But we must not let our interest in our illustration turn us aside from our main theme. We are seeking to show that in the struggle between the radical and the conservative principles in the message of Paul the right is not always on the radical side. The radical demand of an absolute ethic in the midst of a sinful situation may be a sinful demand.

The statement of this principle must be made because the principle is sound. Those who ignore it will come to grief on the facts of life. But the great danger in the principle is that it may be used as the basis for sinful compromises with the unchristian elements of the social order. Many of our compromises with the social order are sinful compromises that should be branded as attempts to avoid the meaning of Christianity in our life situation. Many of our compromises are motivated only by personal greed, or class pride, or racial arrogance. Such sinful compromises must be clearly distinguished from an honest seeking of the word of God for us as we must live in the midst of the orders of our society.

This brings us again to the place of historical decision. The Christian witness never becomes a real witness until it is actualized in the definite choices of life. As Karl Barth writes, "True witnessing to Jesus Christ occurs necessarily in the *unity* of two things, a definite repetition of the confession of Him as the One who has come to us as the Son of God and will come again, and of *the actualizing of this confession in definite decisions*

*in relation to those contemporary questions which agi-
tate the Church and the world."* [22] There must always
be an element of repetition in the Christian witness.
The church speaks in the present situation because of
the inner necessity of her own life. But there has been
an atmosphere of unreality about much of the witness
of the church just because the church has been unwill-
ing to actualize her witness in definite decisions "in relation to contemporary questions which agitate the
church and the world."

It was easy for the early Christians to repeat their
faith in the deity of Christ. But when the apostolic
church was faced by the emperor worship of Rome, the
Christians had to actualize their witness in a definite
decision. They had to say that the worship of the emperor involved in it a denial of the deity of Jesus Christ
and that no Christian could burn incense to the emperor and remain loyal to Jesus Christ.

We find an example of a similar decision as Barth
writes concerning National Socialism, "It has to be seen
and said that here, in National Socialism is an anti-
Church fundamentally hostile to Christianity, and a fundamental dissolution of the just State, it must become
clear in the concrete actualization of the witnessing to
Jesus Christ with which the church is commissioned,
that there has to be a *choice* between faith in Jesus Christ
and the affirmation of the internal and external sover-
eignty of National Socialism, because they are mutually

[22] From: *The Church and the Political Problem of Our Day* by Karl
Barth, page 12. By permission of Charles Scribner's Sons, publishers.
Italics mine.

exclusive, and between them there can be no peace." [23]

Christians in America can approve of the decisions of the early church or the decisions of the church in Germany. What they would like to avoid is decision with regard to the contemporary questions which agitate the church and the state in America. All of us wish to avoid the agony of decision. We wish particularly to avoid decisions concerning the problems which are really vital in our age. There are many problems concerning which the church would be wise to keep silence. But there are also situations in which the church must speak if she is not to be disloyal to her Lord. The church in America needs to hear Barth's warning to "look and see whether she is not now really, of necessity, compromising herself, i.e. compromising herself with the Devil, to whom no ally is dearer than a Church, so absorbed in caring for her good reputation and clean garments, that she keep eternal silence, is eternally meditating, eternally discussing, eternally neutral, a Church so troubled about the transcendence of the Kingdom of God—a thing which isn't really so easy to menace!—that she has become a dumb dog. This is just the thing which must not take place—must not take place today." [24]

A church that is loyal to her Lord cannot avoid the necessity of making decisions concerning the will of God for her in the actual historical situation in which

---

[23] From: *The Church and the Political Problem of Our Day,* by Karl Barth, page 57. By permission of Charles Scribner's Sons, publishers.

[24] From: *The Church and the Political Problem of Our Day,* by Karl Barth, page 21. By permission of Charles Scribner's Sons, publishers.

she finds herself. This decision will grow out of her understanding both of the radical and the conservative principles in her message. But it will be a real decision. It will be that which as a church she must say is her understanding of the will of God in the midst of her contemporary situation. If Christianity is to have anything relevant to say to our world it must proclaim a message that dares to interpret the meaning of being a Christian in the midst of the strange new world which confronts the Christian today.

CHAPTER IV

The Social Implications of Paul's Thought of God

✦ ✦

"THE ultimate question which determines the character of a man or of a civilization is the kind of God that a man worships or that men collectively worship." [1] If these words of Oldham's are true, it is obvious that any study of the social message of the church must inevitably be concerned with theology—with the kind of God that men worship. This concern is inescapable because the character of a civilization is determined by the kind of God that is worshipped in that civilization.

The Apostle Paul was probably the first man to believe in utter seriousness in the one God, the Lord of the whole earth. We do not mean, of course, that Paul was the first apostle of monotheism. The belief in one God has never received more superb statement than in some of the passages of Isaiah. But the prophets did not enter upon a missionary career in which they sought to destroy idolatry and to lead all men and all nations to acknowledge the one God as their Lord and their Saviour. The faith of Paul was not fundamentally different from the faith of the other apostles. But Paul was

---

[1] Oldham, *The Student World*, 1935, page 377. By permission of the editors.

the apostle to the Gentiles. It was under his leadership that Christianity entered upon her world mission.

We need to remember, too, that Paul sought to do more than spread the gospel of Jesus over the whole earth. He preached an exclusive gospel. The Romans did not object to the worship of a new god. But Paul was not content for Jesus to be accorded a place in the pantheon. He was determined that men should worship only the God and Father of our Lord Jesus Christ. Consider in this connection Paul's great statement of the Christian insight concerning all idolatry. "We know that no idol is anything in the world, and that there is no God but one. For though there be that are called gods, whether in heaven or on earth; as there are gods many, and lords many; yet to us there is one God, the Father, of whom are all things, and we unto him; and one Lord, Jesus Christ, through whom are all things, and we through him. Howbeit there is not in all men that knowledge." [2]

Paul is the great apostle of monotheism. He knows that there is but one God. He knows where this one God has revealed Himself. He is confident that the one God has revealed Himself through the one Mediator, the man Jesus Christ.[3]

---

[2] I Corinthians 8:4-7.

[3] I Timothy 2:5.

In quoting the pastoral epistles as Pauline, we do not pronounce judgment on the critical questions involved in the debate as to the authorship of these epistles. All critics will agree that these letters have come out of the early Christian community and that we find in them a record of that process of adjustment between the church and society which is also set forth in the undisputed letters of Paul. In this book, we will refer to these letters as Pauline without raising this question again.

The relevance of this faith of Paul in the midst of the modern world is understood when we realize that the most amazing phenomenon of modern times is the breakdown of monotheism and the return to the ancient conception of tribal gods who are assumed to be identified with the peculiar interests of their worshippers. This breakdown is not always obvious on the surface. Men may continue to call the Being they worship God. They may persist in asserting their faith in monotheism. But if the kind of God whom men worship is thought of in a different way in each nation which worships Him, monotheism is surrendered even if all these nations continue to profess their faith in the one God.

Over against all belief in polytheism there stands Israel's assertion that there is but one only, the living and true God. A serious assertion of monotheism should always lead to a universal faith. If we believe that there is but one God, then this one God must be the God of the whole earth. The inevitable connection between monotheism and a universal faith is found in the great prophets of Israel, especially in Isaiah. Consider, for example, this passage from the forty-fifth chapter of Isaiah. "I am Jehovah; and there is none else. . . . I, Jehovah . . . and there is no God else besides me. . . . Look unto me, and be ye saved, *all* the ends of the earth; for I am God and there is none else. By myself have I sworn, the word is gone forth from my mouth in righteousness, and shall not return, that unto me *every* knee shall bow, *every* tongue shall swear." [4] If

---

[4] Isaiah 45:18, 21-23.

there are many gods, every nation can have its own god. But when men come to believe that there is only one GOD, then they are inevitably driven to the conclusion that this GOD must be the GOD of all men everywhere.

The same close association between monotheism and a universal faith that we find in Isaiah is also found in the writings of Paul. We have already quoted Paul's statement of his faith in the one God and the one Mediator. But in order that we may appreciate the connection between Paul's monotheism and his conception of a universal faith, we need to quote the whole passage in which this statement is found. "This is good and acceptable in the sight of God our Saviour; who would have *all* men to be saved, and come to the knowledge of the truth. For there is one God, one mediator also between God and men, himself man, Christ Jesus, who gave himself a ransom for *all;* the testimony to be borne in its own times; whereunto I was appointed a preacher and an apostle (I speak the truth, I lie not), a teacher of the Gentiles in faith and truth." [5]

Both Paul and Isaiah believe in monotheism. Both of them see the connection between monotheism and a universal faith. But Paul knows that he stands at that moment in history in which the God who has revealed Himself in Israel is ready to reveal Himself to the whole earth. Isaiah knows that the ends of the earth can find salvation in the God of Israel. But Paul knows that he is commissioned to proclaim a gospel that is for all men everywhere. In Paul, Israel's monotheism has become

---

[5] I Timothy 2:3-7.

a crusading faith which is bent upon the conquest of the whole earth.

The three great monotheistic faiths are Judaism, Christianity, and Mohammedanism. All three of these would agree in the assertion that there is only one God. The Jew says, "Hear, O Israel, Jehovah our God is one Jehovah." The Mohammedan says, "There is no God but Allah." The Christian says, "There is but one only, the living and true God." The point of divergence comes when we seek to say where this one God has revealed Himself. The Mohammedan says, "There is no God but Allah, and *Mohammed is his prophet.*" Paul says, "There is one God, *one mediator also between God and men, himself man, Christ Jesus.*"

The clash between Christianity and Mohammedanism is irreconcilable because the God who reveals Himself through the one Mediator, Himself man, Christ Jesus, can by no stretch of the imagination be identified with the god whom Mohammed reveals. If we are ready to say with Paul that there is one God and that the one Mediator between God and man is Christ Jesus, then we must be ready also to say that the god whom Mohammed proclaimed was no god but an idol, a false god.

Christianity and Judaism have the same roots. Paul was intensely a Jew. All the roots of his life went back into the Jewish faith. But it is at the point of Jesus Christ that Christianity and Judaism divide. When Jesus stood before the Sanhedrin, the high priest said unto Him, "I adjure thee by the living God, that thou tell us whether thou art the Christ, the Son of God." And

Jesus said, "I am." [6] The claim of Jesus was pronounced blasphemy. The Jews would agree with Paul that there was one God. They would not agree that the God who spoke unto their fathers through the prophets by divers portions and in divers manners had given the final revelation of Himself to them in His Son, Jesus—the Christ.

As Christians, we affirm that the God who spoke to us through the prophets is the God who came to us in Jesus Christ. We believe that the light of the knowledge of the glory of God is found in the face of Jesus Christ. Because of this we must declare that Judaism is inadequate.

In Paul the universalism of Christianity and the particularism of Judaism have met. Paul knows that salvation is of the Jews. He knows that the Jews were "intrusted with the oracles of God." [7] He knows that he belongs to a Messianic people who were chosen to be the vehicle of God's revelation of Himself to the world. Of Israel, Paul can write, "I have great sorrow and unceasing pain in my heart. For I could wish that I myself were anathema from Christ for my brethren's sake, my kinsmen according to the flesh: who are the Israelites; whose is the adoption, and the glory, and the covenants, and the giving of the law, and the service of God, and the promises; of whom is Christ as concerning the flesh, who is over all, God blessed for ever." [8]

The Jews were a Messianic people. They were the

<hr />

[6] Mark 14:62; Matthew 26:63.

[7] Romans 3:2.

[8] Romans 9:2-5.

bearers of a revelation. When the Jews were confronted by the great apostle to the Gentiles they faced their day of supreme opportunity. The rejection of Christ by the rulers of the Jewish nation need not have resulted in His rejection by the Jews as a whole. When the Jews faced Paul, the moment in history had come when the Jews were asked to rise to their God-given destiny. They were asked to lose themselves in the larger stream of Christian life. They refused, and in their refusal they missed their great opportunity. They were disloyal to the insights of their great prophets. They refused to be the mediums of a purpose of God that reached out to the whole earth. They fell back into the particularism of Judaism. They believed in the one God, but they were not willing to embrace a faith through which the God of Israel was to become the God of the whole earth.

The relevance of the ideas we have been presenting can be seen at once when we leave the sphere of history and enter the arena of contemporary life. The modern world has fallen away from monotheism and has turned to tribal gods. What has happened in our world is that men have made themselves gods after their own image and according to their own lusts. In Russian Communism, we have a messianic class whose cosmic hour has rung. In National Socialism, there is a Holy Germany whose god is identified with the blood and soil of the German people. In Fascism, we have the deification of the Holy Roman Empire. In Japan, the nation is centered around a Holy Family who are the descendants of the Sun-Goddess, a family to whom there is given the mission to rule the world. All of these faiths have in common the fact that they have taken a partial element in human life and deified it.

Whatever else we may say about these faiths, it is evident that all of them agree in the denial of the Christian religion. Christianity proclaims the absolute. Christianity asserts that in the ONE MEDIATOR the absolute has entered history. All false absolutes know that they are inevitably called in question by the proclamation of the true absolute. All of these religions know that their most deadly enemy is Christianity. Between these faiths and a true understanding of the message of Paul there can be no compromise. If the God we know in Jesus Christ is the true God, then the god who meets us in these systems is a false god, an idol, a man-god, a creation of the minds of men.

Against the background of this thought, we can understand Karl Barth's indictment of National Socialism. "Why talk of an anti-Church fundamentally hostile to Christianity? I would reply: because in what one would call the deity of National Socialism—the National Socialist myth, the God whom the Christian Church serves is absolutely and in principle unrecognizable; and because in the self-absolutising life of National Socialist man the Christian life which finds its consolation and hope in Jesus Christ, is absolutely and in principle unrecognizable. National Socialism has for its part long since declared by both word and deed that it is absolute and in principle unable to recognize either its own deity in Him whom the church calls God, or its

own life in the Christian life. . . . In the innermost and
real and most holy essence of National Socialism, in its
mystical faith and not in any 'excrescences,' there has
entered the field not just another god, not just a strange
god, but a hostile god, an evil god, and a hostile, evil
service of god." [9]

The study of theology is not irrelevant to those who
would deal with the social life of man. In the clash of
the great social systems today we have at bottom a clash
of theologies. These competing social systems do not
agree in their theology. If they are at war with Christianity they are also at war with each other. The god
who is revealed in "the blood and soil" of the German
people cannot be identified with the god who is worshipped through obedience to the holy family of Japan.
If the world was given over to these systems, their final
effect would be to destroy completely the idea of monotheism and leave us with a series of tribal gods very
similar to the tribal gods of the ancient world. In these
systems we have returned to a practical polytheism.

The religions of the false gods possess no unifying
principle which would enable them to unite in the
building of a new world. All that they possess in common is common hatreds. Men can be unified by hatred
as they seek to destroy that which they hate. But those
who have been unified by a common hatred are certain
to fall to fighting among themselves as soon as that
which they hate has been destroyed. And men who
have been united by hatred can never co-operate as they

[9] From: *The Church and the Political Problem of Our Day,* by Karl
Barth, pages 48-50. By permission of Charles Scribner's Sons, publishers.

seek to build a new world. When men begin to build they declare their loves. And those who have nothing in common which they love cannot build together a new civilization. A world that was divided between the National Socialism of Germany, the Fascism of Italy, and the Emperor Worship of Japan would be a world that was given over to the most terrible forms of idolatry.

But you cannot face Communism, or Fascism, or National Socialism, or Emperor Worship with armies alone. The real conflict between them and Christianity is a conflict of theologies, and against them Christianity must develop a theology that has crusading power. As Nicholas Berdyaev says, "Only a mobilization of the spirit can be set against the modern collective insanity and demoniac possession, against modern polydemonism and idolatry. Social organization alone is powerless to struggle against this chaotic decay of the world and of man. The world threatens to become an organized and technicized chaos in which only the most terrible forms of idolatry and demon-worship can live. Once again, man must return to monotheism, or else degenerate, be resolved into cosmic elements compulsorily organized into social collectives. . . . A new Christian piety must be revealed in our world. And upon this new Christian piety depends the fate of the world and that of man." [10]

"The world must return to monotheism or perish."

---

[10] From: *The Fate of Man in the Modern World*, by Nicholas Berdyaev, page 123. Published by The Student Christian Movement, London, in The Religion and Life Series.

Nicholas Berdyaev did not name the kind of monotheism to which the world must return but we know enough of his thoughts to know that it was the monotheism of Paul. "There is one God, one mediator also between God and men, himself man, Christ Jesus." The world must return to that monotheism in which the one God is acknowledged as the One who has given the full and final revelation of His character and His will for man in the God-man, Christ Jesus.

CHAPTER V

The Social Implications of Paul's Thought of Man

✦ ✦

"THE central theme of our epoch is that of all history—the fate of man. What is taking place in the world today is not a crisis of humanism (that is a topic of secondary importance), but the crisis of humanity. We face the question, is that being to whom the future belongs to be called man, as previously, or something other? We are witnessing the process of dehumanization in all phases of culture and of social life. Above all, moral consciousness is being dehumanized. Man has ceased to be the supreme value: he has ceased to have any value at all. . . . The image of God in man is being darkened; man is losing the sense, which Christianity revealed to him, of being a son of God. . . .

"The problem of Christian anthropology, the religious question of mankind, is the basic problem of our epoch. And only the fulness of Christian truth can fight successfully against dehumanization, and prevent the final destruction of man. The world tried to affirm man as against Christianity and arrived at a negation of man himself. And outside Christianity, or better, outside of Christ, there is no salvation for fallen man. To a renewed and transfigured Christianity man must now address himself for protection. This is the only defense for human dignity and freedom and creativity, for man's humanity to man. Only Christianity can create an inner society; what all the social movements produce is external." [1]

These quotations from Berdyaev are sufficient to bring before us the tremendous importance in the midst of the contemporary social situation of a Christian anthropology. We have seen that behind the social systems that are competing for the mastery of our world there is a struggle of theologies. We have seen that the inevitable struggle between them and Christianity is that the god who is revealed in these systems cannot be identified with the God who comes to us in Jesus Christ. But it is equally true to say that the conflicts of our generation center in anthropology. Behind the various social systems there are diverging answers as to the meaning and value of man in the universe. In some cases, the conflict of anthropologies is more obvious than the conflict of theologies. Russian Communism, for example, might not be willing to admit that it had a theology. (Although it could hardly deny that it had absolutized itself and become a religion.) But no system that commands the loyalties of men can avoid having an anthropology. We cannot attempt the reconstruction of the life of man unless we have for our guidance some conception of the meaning of man's life in our universe. And no anthropology which leaves out of account the spiritual life of man can permanently

---

[1] From: *The Fate of Man in the Modern World,* by Nicholas Berdyaev, pages 26, 33, 121. Published by The Student Christian Movement in The Religion and Life Series.

satisfy the human heart or provide a basis upon which an abiding society can be built.

Paul has a theology. Has he an anthropology which is adequate for the needs of our world? In outlining the anthropology of Paul, we have no desire to set his anthropology off as distinct from the rest of the New Testament. Our interest is in the Christian anthropology as a whole. But it is true that in the writings of Paul we find a splendid expression of that view of man which underlies the whole Bible.

Brunner is right in his contention that man must be understood from the top down if he is to be understood as a whole. Our knowledge of man should include a knowledge of his physical life. The whole field of medicine is concerned with the physical life of man. But man cannot be understood merely on the basis of the study of the structure of his body.

Man is a creature whose existence is dependent upon food, shelter, clothing. No one would deny the need for an adequate economic basis of life. Man cannot live without bread but man cannot live by bread alone. The Marxian understanding of man has in it a measure of truth. The life of culture must rest upon a basis in economics. The blessings of freedom may become meaningless to men if for them freedom is merely the freedom to starve. But the problems of economics can never be solved on the basis of economics alone.

Man is a sexual being. The principle of sex runs through the whole of human life. And the overemphasis on sex by men such as Freud may be rooted in a reaction against the failure of men in the past to under-

stand the importance of sex in the life of man. But the
principle of sex cannot be made the key to the whole
of life. Man cannot find abiding satisfaction in the sexual life unless this element of the life of man is rooted
in a higher view of man that sets sexual desire in its
proper place in life as a whole.

Man is a creature. There is a kinship between man
and the animal world. But the idea of evolution does
not seriously challenge the Christian faith unless men
seek to use it to build an anthropology, a philosophy of
man and his place in the universe.

Man must be understood from the top down. His
economic life, his sexual life, even his moral life, must
be related to an understanding of man as a child of
God. It is our purpose therefore to set over against the
various understandings of man that prevail in the modern world the Biblical view of man, with a special emphasis on the thought of man that is found in Paul.

The writers of the Bible feel the problem of man in
the universe. The psalmist asks,

> "When I consider thy heavens, the work of thy fingers,
> The moon and the stars, which thou hast ordained;
> What is man, that thou art mindful of him?
> And the son of man, that thou visitest him?" [2]

The answer of the Bible to the question, *What is
Man?*, is that God created man in His own image. Man
is a creature. He belongs to the order of created beings.
It is the fact of creation that marks the chasm between
God and man. God is the Uncreated. Man is the crea-

---

[2] Psalm 8:3, 4.

ture of God. But it is also the fact of creation that binds God and man together. *Man is God's because God has made him.*

> "Know ye that Jehovah, he is God:
> It is he that hath made us, and we are his:
> We are his people, and the sheep of his pasture."[3]

God has made man in His own image. We cannot enter at this time into all of those debates in which men have sought to define the image of God in man. According to Brunner, the image of God in man is man's capacity to hear (or not to hear) the word of God. Man is a creature who can hear the word of God. God can speak to him. All of those things that are distinctive in man are related to his capacity to hear the word of God. With the capacity to hear the word of God, there must go a limited amount of freedom. With the gift of freedom there goes the element of responsibility which marks man as distinct from the animal world. And with the gift of freedom and responsibility, there is also the possibility of sin. With the capacity to hear the word of God, there is also the capacity not to hear the word of God.

The difference between man and the rest of the creation of God can be seen if we think of a man who has placed his infant son in the midst of a room that is filled with marionettes. The marionettes will move when he pulls the strings. They will speak when he speaks through them. They will never be out of harmony with his will. They will never break his heart.

---

[3] Psalm 100:3.

But the infant in the midst of the marionettes has a capacity the wooden dolls will never have. The child has the capacity to hear his father's word and to answer his father in the speech of men.

Man is not independent of God. He is made to find the center of his life in God. But man is different from all the other creatures upon our earth in that man and man alone is made in the image of God. This is the view of man that we find in the Bible.

Man has sinned. Man who is created in the image of God has refused to find the center of his life in God. Man has rejected the word of God. Sin brings death. The Bible knows that all of our human life is existence unto death. The characteristic of all earthly life is that it is moving unto death. Death is the last enemy of mankind, and the ultimate affirmation of man that is found in the Bible lies beyond the grave.

We have presented briefly the Biblical view of man without an attempt to support it by quotations from the Bible and without any effort to show that these ideas are part of the message of Paul. It now becomes our purpose to show that this view is expressed by Paul. Paul is aware that God is the Creator and Sustainer of all life. In his speech to the Athenians, he says, "The God that made the world and all things therein, he, being Lord of heaven and earth, dwelleth not in temples made with hands; neither is he served by men's hands, as though he needed anything, seeing he himself giveth to all life, and breath, and all things; and he made of one every nation of men to dwell on all the face of the earth, having determined their appointed seasons, and the bounds of their habitation; that they should seek God, if haply they might feel after him and find him, though he is not far from each one of us: for in him we live, and move, and have our being."[4]

Paul expresses the idea of creation also in Colossians. In this passage Paul is writing to a Christian group and he makes it clear that Jesus Christ is the agent of creation. "For in him [Christ] were all things created, in the heavens and upon the earth, things visible and things invisible . . . all things have been created through him, and unto him; and he is before all things, and in him all things consist."[5]

Paul knows the terrible reality of sin as it permeates all of human life. The description of man that he gives in the first chapter of Romans, verses 18-32, is one of the darkest pictures that has ever been painted of the sin of the human race. This picture has not come from the pen of an idealist who has never faced the depths of evil that can be found in human life.

Paul knows also the solidarity of man in sin. Of both the Jews and the Greeks he says that "they are *all* under sin." He quotes with approval from the Fourteenth Psalm.

"There is none righteous, no, not one:
 There is none that understandeth,
 There is none that seeketh after God;
 They have all turned aside, they are together become un-
     profitable;
 There is none that doeth good, no, not so much as one."[6]

---

[4] Acts 17:24-27.
[5] Colossians 1:16, 17.
[6] Romans 3:11, 12.

He asserts the universal sinfulness of man, "that *every* mouth may be stopped, and *all* the world may be brought under the judgment of God." [7]

Paul boldly declares the responsibility of man in sin, a responsibility that extends both to those within the sphere of revelation and to those who are judged by the light that they have apart from revelation. "There is no respect of persons with God. For as many as have sinned without the law shall also perish without the law: and as many as have sinned under the law shall be judged by the law . . . for when Gentiles that have not the law do by nature the things of the law, these, not having the law, are the law unto themselves; in that they show the work of the law written in their hearts, their conscience bearing witness therewith, and their thoughts one with another accusing or else excusing them." [8]

Over against this dark picture Paul is confident that he is the bearer of a message of redemption that is available to all who will receive it. "For I am not ashamed of the gospel: for it is the power of God unto salvation to every one that believeth; to the Jew first, and also to the Greek. For therein is revealed a righteousness of God from faith unto faith: as it is written, But the righteous shall live by faith." [9]

Paul's message of redemption was not with him an untried theory. Most of his life was spent in the proclamation of the gospel. He was conscious of a power at work in the world through which men could be re-

---

[7] Romans 3:19.
[8] Romans 2:11, 12, 14, 15.
[9] Romans 1:16, 17.

deemed. He writes to the Corinthians, "Be not deceived: neither fornicators, nor idolaters, nor adulterers, nor effeminate, nor abusers of themselves with men, nor thieves, nor covetous, nor drunkards, nor revilers, nor extortioners, shall inherit the kingdom of God. And *such* were *some* of *you:* but ye were washed, but ye were sanctified, but ye were justified in the name of the Lord Jesus Christ, and in the Spirit of our God." [10]

He prays for the Ephesians to know "the exceeding greatness of his power to us-ward who believe, according to that working of the strength of his might which he wrought in Christ, when he raised him from the dead." [11] He continues, "And you did he make alive, when ye were dead through your trespasses and sins, wherein ye once walked according to the course of this world . . . but God, being rich in mercy, for his great love wherewith he loved us, even when we were dead through our trespasses, made us alive together with Christ . . . that in the ages to come he might show the exceeding riches of his grace in kindness toward us in Christ Jesus." [12]

The closing sentence of the paragraph we have just quoted leads us inevitably forward to the culmination of Paul's anthropology, his doctrine of the goal of man. Paul knows that in the creation of man God has begun a work which is not finished. "Man remains in the workshop of God." Paul knows that through creation and redemption God is moving on to the FINISHED MAN.

---

[10] I Corinthians 6:9-11.
[11] Ephesians 1:19, 20.
[12] Ephesians 2:1-5, 7.

44328

This goal is set forth in Ephesians. Paul speaks of the gifts God has given His servants "for the perfecting of the saints, unto the work of ministering, unto the building up of the body of Christ: *till we all attain unto the unity of the faith, and of the knowledge of the Son of God, unto a fullgrown man, unto the measure of the stature* of the fulness of Christ." [13]

In commenting on verse 13, Robinson says, "Till we all come . . . unto a perfect man.[14] That is all of us together (for this is implied by the Greek) to God's New Man, grown at length to full manhood. Not to 'perfect man'; for the Apostle uses the plural of the lower state only: 'that we be no longer children' is his own contrast. We are to grow out of our individualism unto the corporate oneness of the fullgrown Man.— *In the New Man, grown to perfect manhood, St. Paul finds the consummation of human life.*" [15]

Paul presents here both the goal for the individual and the goal for the human race. The individual who is in Christ has been laid hold of by the power of God. The goal of the redemptive process is that he shall come to the measure of the stature of the fulness of Christ. Paul would tell the individual Christian that he has been laid hold of by God and that he will be kept by God until at last God's work in him is finished and he has been brought to the measure of the stature of the

[13] Ephesians 4:12, 13.
[14] Robinson bases his commentary on the King James Version. The quotation above is from the American Standard Version.
[15] *Commentary on Ephesians*, Macmillan. Second Edition, 1922, page 100. Used by permission. Italics mine.

fulness of Christ. For the Christian there can be no higher goal for character than to become like Christ.

But Paul's thought in this passage is essentially social. He is thinking not so much of individuals as of man as a unity. He has his eye fixed on the FINISHED MAN, on the ultimate goal toward which the whole process of creation and redemption is moving. Paul is thinking of the completed body of Christ, of the FINISHED MAN who will continue through the ages when the whole temporal process has been brought to an end.

The goal Paul sets for MAN is beyond the crisis of death. All of earthly life is still in the midst of an existence unto death. But it is Paul's goal that gives to our earthly life meaning and value. In Paul's thinking man is far more than a creature who is formed out of the dust of the earth. Man is made in the image of God. He has the possibility of an eternal destiny. Man is a creature of earth, but he who has borne the image of the earthy may also bear the image of the heavenly. Man is mortal, but he may put on immortality. Man is corruptible, but he may put on incorruption. Man lives in an existence unto death, but death may be swallowed up in victory.

Paul believes in the origin of man as created by God in His own image. He knows the fall of man and the prevalence of sin. He knows the goal of man. In his thinking there is an adequate goal for the individual and for the race. Between man in his origin and man in his final goal there is Paul's doctrine of the call. Paul knows that man in his earthly life is confronted by the word of God in Jesus Christ. Paul's conviction is that in man, even in fallen man, there is the capacity to hear or not to hear this word.

This conviction of Paul's is in harmony with his own experience. As he was on the road to Damascus, Jesus Christ met him and conquered him. As he looks back over his life, Paul is able to say, "I was not disobedient unto the heavenly vision."[16] But Paul is convinced that in content if not in form his experience is possible to every man. Through the preaching of the church, Jesus Christ confronts men and sets them in decision. As he says in Romans, "The word is nigh thee, in thy mouth, and in thy heart: that is, the word of faith, which we preach: because if thou shalt confess with thy mouth Jesus as Lord, and shalt believe in thy heart that God raised him from the dead, thou shalt be saved. . . . For the scripture saith, Whosoever believeth on him shall not be put to shame. For there is no distinction between Jew and Greek: for the same Lord is Lord of all, and is rich unto all that call upon him: *for, Whosoever shall call upon the name of the Lord shall be saved.*" [17]

But Paul knows also that *men can refuse to hear the call of God*. And the great passage in which he sets forth the call is followed by a passage in which he wrestles with the problem of unbelief and closes with the picture of God as all day long He spreads out His hands to a disobedient and gainsaying people.[18]

It is the call of God that sets us in decision. It is the call of God that makes individuals out of us. The call

---

[16] Acts 26:19.
[17] Romans 10:8, 9, 11-13.
[18] Romans 10:21.

of love is always intensely personal. And in his response to God's call of love man either finds the center of his life in God or refuses to find the true center of his life and falls away to his idols. Through the call, God overcomes the isolation of the individual and sets the individual Christian within the community of the church. The very word church is the translation of the Greek word, *"ecclesia,"* which means the "called out."

In the call of God the isolation of man is overcome, and the individual is set within the living fellowship of the body of Christ on earth.

It may seem that a statement of Paul's anthropology is out of place in a study of his social message. There has been very little of direct concern with the social struggle in the pages of this chapter. But if the question of man is the central question of our epoch, then it is essential in any understanding of Paul's social thought for us to have a clear understanding of the view of man that is inherent in all of Paul's thinking. If only the fulness of Christian truth can fight against the false anthropologies of the day, then it is essential that we know the Christian understanding of man. If Paul's understanding of man is true, then the Marxian understanding of man cannot be true. We must have a true anthropology to save us from the false anthropologies.

When we have understood Paul's view of man, there are two things we must say, and when we have said these things we have returned to a direct concern with the social struggle. The first comment we must make is that any view of man which leaves unconsidered the great questions with which Paul wrestles must in the long run prove hopelessly inadequate for the needs of mankind. Men must inevitably ask such questions as, Where do we come from? Why are we here? Where are we going? Man has a sense of creaturehood, and he must inevitably ask concerning the Creator. Man has a sense of sin and failure, and he must seek for a message of redemption from sin. Man knows that he is mortal, and he must seek for victory over death. Men are lonely, and they must yearn for some abiding basis of community life. In times of desperate need, we may absolutize a partial view of man, but in the end its inadequacy will be discovered, and men will seek again an anthropology which has a positive answer to the deepest questions of human existence.

Our second comment is that a Christian understanding of man that fails to concern itself with the whole of human life has proved disloyal to Christ. Man must be understood from the top down and not from the bottom up. But we must not have a Christian message which is interested in the saving of the souls of men and is unconcerned about feeding their bodies.

In the Christian faith, man who is a child of God must have both the will and the power to order his economic life in the interests of all of God's children and not for the enrichment of a favored few. In a sense, the false anthropologies are a judgment upon the church. We would not have had the Marxian understanding of man if Christians had had a proper concern for the economic welfare of all men. We would never have had Fascism if the church in generations past had dealt adequately with racial arrogance and national selfishness.

The only anthropology that can save our world is a Christian anthropology which deals fearlessly with the whole life of man.[19]

---

[19] As a contribution to the study of anthropology, we are fortunate in having two major books that have been published in recent years. They are: *Man in Revolt,* by Emil Brunner, 1939, and *The Nature and Destiny of Man,* by Reinhold Niebuhr, 1941. Both books were published by Charles Scribner's Sons.

CHAPTER VI

The Order of Sex—Man and Woman

✦ ✦

THE fact of sex is an order of creation. In the biological facts of sex, there is the God-given basis for the preservation and propagation of the human species. Out of this order of creation there has developed in the history of mankind the institution of the family. While the customs that are connected with marriage and the family life have varied greatly in the history of the world, there has been in every society something that would correspond to the institution of the family. Through the union of man and woman, children are born into the world, and in the life of the home these children are cared for until they are able to take their place in the life of society.

In the Graeco-Roman world within which he moved, Paul found that the institution of the family had achieved to a high degree of historical development. The family was the basic social institution. As Paul sought to advise his converts concerning their life in the midst of society, he was inevitably forced to define their attitude toward the home. This involved, of course, a discussion of the Christian view of marriage. A discussion of marriage would lead at once to a discussion of those sins of sex through which the marriage relation was violated. The institution of the family probably affected the lives of Paul's converts more deeply than any other social institution. For this reason it was doubly important that there should be a clear understanding of the Christian view of marriage and the family life.[1]

In his setting of a high standard of sexual purity within the church, Paul is faced by a double problem. In many cases, his converts were gathered from a decaying pagan society in which the standards of purity were very low. And in his attempt to free the Christian from bondage to the law, Paul was always faced with the danger that his converts would turn their new freedom into license. But in spite of these difficulties, Paul is utterly uncompromising in his demand for sexual purity among the members of his churches.

In the fifth and sixth chapters of I Corinthians, Paul deals with the sin of fornication. He starts with a specific instance in which a man who has been guilty of the sin of incest has been permitted to remain in the fellowship of the church. But his teaching is general as well as specific, and in these chapters he gives us the basis upon which he must have dealt with this sin whenever it appeared in his churches.

He reminds the Corinthians that a little leaven leavens the whole lump.[2] By this he means that when sins of this kind are tolerated unrebuked within the fellowship of the church they will inevitably spread. For this reason, the Christians at Corinth are told to "have no

---

[1] In our chapter on the radical and conservative principles in Paul, we have already discussed Paul's treatment of men and women as equal before God and Paul's toleration of the subordination of woman to man in the midst of Roman society. See pages 57, 58, 67-70.

[2] I Corinthians 5:6.

company with fornicators." [3] By this Paul does not mean that Christians are to have no dealings with men in the world whose sexual lives are impure. Such a demand would have been impossible in Paul's world. He does mean that within the fellowship of the church there must be the refusal to keep company "if any man that is named a brother be a fornicator."

He lays down the general principle that the unrighteous shall not inherit the kingdom of God. In order that no one can misunderstand him, he lists some sins that he considers inconsistent with the living of the Christian life. Among these he includes the sins of sex. "Be not deceived: neither fornicators, . . . nor adulterers, nor effeminate, nor abusers of themselves with men . . . shall inherit the kingdom of God." [4] By this Paul does not mean that men who have been guilty of such sins cannot be saved. He makes it clear in verse 11 that the church in Corinth has in it many who through Christ have found salvation from these and similar sins. What Paul means is that men cannot at the same time be Christian and continue in these sins.

In verses 12-19 of the sixth chapter of I Corinthians, Paul gives us his reasons for holding that these sins of sex are inconsistent with genuine Christian living. In verse 12, he tells them that they enjoy the freedom of the Christian, but he reminds them that in the exercise of their freedom they are to be masters of the body and not to be mastered by the body.

Verse 13 of this chapter reads, "Meats for the belly,

[3] I Corinthians 5:9.
[4] I Corinthians 6:9.

and the belly for meats: but God shall bring to nought both it and them. But the body is not for fornication, but for the Lord; and the Lord for the body." In commenting on this verse Goudge says, "Here Paul begins to deal with the second ground on which the fornication was defended. It was argued, and it is argued still, that the body is for sexual intercourse, just as the belly is for meats, i.e. that in each case there is a natural correspondence and adaptation, which it is folly to ignore. St. Paul replies that the analogy is a false one. The belly is for meats and for them alone; it serves no higher purpose; it is an organ which belongs only to man's life here, and no more has an immortality before it, than the meats with which it deals. Quite otherwise is it with the body as a whole. . . . It is for the Lord to serve Him, either as the instrument of service or as the instrument of sacrifice.[5] On the other hand the Lord is for the body. He, Incarnate and Glorified, true man and true God, is the perfect answer to the true needs of that body, which He takes even here into true union with Himself, and will one day raise and glorify."[6]

In further comment on this passage as a whole, Goudge continues, "We should notice here St. Paul's profound answer to the plea that impurity is natural. We can only decide the natural use of anything when we know the main purpose which it is intended to serve. It is in the highest sense unnatural to use for a

---

[5] Philippians 1:20; Hebrews 10:5.

[6] From: *Commentary on First Corinthians,* by H. L. Goudge, Fifth Edition Revised, page 48. This commentary is in the Westminster Commentaries and is published by Methuen, 36 Essex Street, London.

low purpose what is intended for a high one, if the lower purpose interferes with the higher. 'The body is for the Lord.' To serve him is its characteristic purpose. Impurity affects the body as a whole, and indeed not only the body. Fornication like marriage brings a man and a woman into a relation so close and powerful, that there may almost be said to be a mingling of personality. As Edwards well says, 'the roots of the union, whether in or out of wedlock, live and grow necessarily in the nature of each.' To form such a union with a harlot must render impossible the carrying out of the true purpose of the body, and sever the higher union with Christ. Individual sins weaken that union, but the Lord's intercession can deal with them (I John 2:1); they are without the body in the sense that they do not fundamentally alter it; but with fornication it is otherwise; the far-reaching consequences of the union between man and woman must either serve God's purpose as they do in Christian marriage, or utterly wreck them. . . . Impurity does not injure the material substance of the body, in a way different from that in which gluttony and drunkenness injure it; indeed it often injures it far less seriously. What it degrades and injures is the personality as a whole." [7]

When we think deeply enough on this subject, we instinctively realize the truth of Paul's position. In fornication there is more than a meeting of the bodies of men and women on a purely animal plane. There is a mutual surrender of their whole personalities. And

[7] From: *Commentary on First Corinthians,* by H. L. Goudge, page 51.

this surrender is in violation of the Christian's surrender of his personality to Jesus Christ. Men and women must choose here. They cannot at the same time yield themselves to Christ and give themselves to the sin of fornication. Those who choose to give themselves to sexual sin are also choosing to destroy their union with Christ.

The interesting thing about Paul's whole argument is that it is just as true and as vital today as it was when he gave it to the church at Corinth. There are many arguments for purity that Paul does not mention. Some of these root in the fear of disease or in the sense of wrong to unborn life. With the advance of medical science, these arguments may cease to be as powerful or as effective as they once were. But Paul's basic position will abide. *In the sin of impurity there is a surrender of our whole personalities that is inconsistent with the Christian's surrender of himself to Jesus Christ.*

Paul has often been thought of as opposed to marriage. This thought is based on some of the statements of Paul in which he advises against marriage.[8] But when we take the impact of Paul's thought as a whole, we cannot say that he is opposed to marriage. In his letter to Timothy, he condemns as heretics those who forbid to marry. In particular he shows here an utter lack of patience with that spirit of asceticism in which so much of the Oriental opposition to marriage was rooted.[9] In the letter to the Corinthians that we are considering, he defends his right to marry and reminds the

---

[8] I Corinthians 7:1, 8, 27, 39, 40.
[9] I Timothy 4:3-5.

Corinthians that Peter and the other apostles and the brothers of Jesus are married.[10]

There are, however, two grounds upon which Paul does at times advise against marriage. The first of these is of a somewhat temporary nature. In I Corinthians 7:26, 27, he says, "I think therefore that this is good by reason of the distress that is upon us, namely, that it is good for a man to be as he is. Art thou bound unto a wife? seek not to be loosed. Art thou loosed from a wife? seek not a wife." As the context shows, these verses are spoken in the light of Paul's expectation of the near return of Christ and the end of the present world order. They are spoken also in the midst of the present distress. Commentators usually interpret this to mean a threatening persecution in which men might feel the need of being free from all other obligations in order that they might not be hindered in their testimony to Christ. While this situation was temporary, it is similar to other situations in which men may choose not to marry because of the *distress* that is upon them.

Paul's second reason for advising against marriage is very close to his first. He realizes that through marriage Christians may come to a place of divided loyalties. He writes, "But I would have you to be free from cares. He that is unmarried is careful for the things of the Lord, how he may please the Lord: but he that is married is careful for the things of the world, how he may please his wife, and is divided. So also the woman that is unmarried and the virgin is careful for the things of the

[10] I Corinthians 9:5.

Lord, that she may be holy both in body and in spirit: but she that is married is careful for the things of the world, how she may please her husband. And this I say for your own profit; not that I may cast a snare upon you, but for that which is seemly, and that ye may attend upon the Lord without distraction." [11]

Everyone will realize that the problem which Paul faces here is a real problem. It is easy to see that Paul in the midst of his roving life as the apostle to the Gentiles would have found it very difficult to combine loyalty to Christ with the obligations of the family life.

Those who marry do assume responsibilities. In this respect, they do not have the freedom of those who are without these responsibilities. But it does not always follow that the Christian life is best realized in the absence of responsibilities. And the testimony of most Christians is that loyalty to the responsibilities of the home does not involve any lack of loyalty to Christ and His church. Christ demands the first loyalty of our life. There is no place in the Christian's life for an idolatry that places love of children ahead of love of Christ. But we do not need to love our children less because we must love Christ more. In fact, when God is placed first, there is a fiber and moral quality about our human loves which they never attain unless they are related to a consuming love for Christ. And through the homes which they have created, Christian men and women have often rendered their largest service to Christ and His kingdom. The decision here must be left to every

[11] I Corinthians 7:32-35.

individual as he faces the demands of his Lord on him. Some may find that they can best serve Christ by not marrying. Others will find that it is within the married life that they can best serve their God.

Paul does offer to the unmarried person that sublimation of life through which the driving energy that is associated with sex is sublimated and made to serve the cause of Christ. The psychologists tell us that it is only through a surrender such as this that those who do not marry are able to find inner peace and power.

But while Paul is aware that for some marriage may lead to a divided loyalty, he is also aware that many Christians will find that it is with the marriage relation that they find freedom from distractions and the full release of life in the service of God. He writes, "But I say to the unmarried and to widows . . . if they have not continency, let them marry: for it is better to marry than to burn." [12] In commenting on this verse Goudge writes, "The exact force of 'have not continency' is not quite clear. Probably St. Paul would include under it all cases where there is a protracted and dangerous struggle. The Greek of the last clause of the verse marks, as the English does not, that something worse than occasional temptations to impurity is meant. The great value of celibacy lies in freedom from distraction in the service of the Lord; when celibacy brings worse distraction than marriage, its value is to a great extent gone." [13]

Some people are able to sublimate their sexual life and find freedom through the celibate life in which

---

[12] I Corinthians 7:8, 9.
[13] From: *Commentary on First Corinthians*, by H. L. Goudge, page 55.

they are able to give all of their energies to the service of God. But Paul realizes that for many the struggle for continency produces a divided life, a life in which much of the energy of life is consumed in the struggle with those passions which should find normal and natural expression in the wedded life. In spite of the inevitable distractions of married life, Paul feels that these people will find in marriage that freedom from internal struggle which will mean that they are able to serve Christ better married than unmarried.

Paul does not consider the celibate life as in itself a holier life than the married life. To Paul the pure love of man and woman is such a holy thing that in the mystical union between man and woman which is realized in marriage he can find the earthly illustration of the mystical union between Christ and His church. He could not have done this if he had felt that there was anything that was degrading in Christian marriage.[14]

The finality of marriage is affirmed in the very fact that Paul can use the union of man and woman in marriage to illustrate the union of Christ with His church. The surrender of the soul to Christ has about it the note of finality. And if it lacks this note it is not genuine. No man can say that he will experiment with being a Christian for a year and that if he does not like it he will at the end of the year return to sin. Jesus Christ would receive no man on such a basis. *We cannot experiment with finalities.* The surrender of the soul to God, if genuine, must be a yielding that is final and irrevocable.

---

[14] See Ephesians 5:22-33 for the working out of this relation.

And in Christian marriage there must be a note of surrender that is final. Once marriage is consummated it must be accepted as final by both parties. And if marriage is entered into on any other basis it lacks the note of finality that is essential to its success. From this point of view, Paul would say that trial marriage is not marriage at all. If marriage lacks in the beginning any note of surrender that is final, it lacks an element that is utterly essential to a Christian view of marriage.

The finality of marriage is involved in the very nature of the mystical union of man and woman which is a part of Christian marriage. In marriage "they two have become one flesh." This sense of oneness which is always present in the love of man and woman at its best is a premonition of the fact that marriage is intended to issue in children and that through the child a man and woman are bound together in a way that cannot be revoked. On this subject, Brunner writes, "The first fact is this: that every human being is irrevocably the child of one man and one woman, that every father, with this woman, and every mother, with this man, is, irrevocably, the father and mother of this child. By this I do not mean the mere biological fact that every living creature has arisen out of an ovum fertilized by semen, but I mean something which does not take place outside of the human sphere, namely that a subject is united with two other subjects in this unparalleled and unique manner, and not only that this is so, but that this subject knows it. The unique element in this human relation is this: that my existence—not my physical existence, my existence as an object, but my human existence—is thus bound up with two other existences. I, as a child, owe my life (not my physical life but my human life) to these two persons. And I, as father or as mother, with this woman or with this man . . . have taken part in the divine miracle of creation. Not a body but a real corporeal person (subject), a human being, now stands there alongside of me as that which has come into being as a result of my being united to this woman. Were this being simply an *object,* once the thing was done we could dissolve partnership and each could go our separate way. But since this being is a subject, just as I am a subject, that is since this process lies beyond all mere causality and objectivity, since I, the father, as well as the mother and the child, know irrevocably that this fact is irrevocable, then we three persons are bound together in a way in which no other three persons have ever been bound together, in an unparalleled and indissoluble relation. The seeing eyes of all three, our mutual knowledge of one another and of this relation, hold us firmly to one another. This does not mean that we could not drift away from each other, but it does mean that should we separate *we would still remain bound to one another because of our knowledge of this indestructible fact which lies at the basis of our existence.*[15] This trinity of being we call the human structure of our existence. It is clear that this is not a biological fact, for—if, for instance, we think of it from the child's point of view—*if the father and mother separate, the child feels that the bottom has fallen out*

---

[15] Italics mine.

of his existence.[16] He sees the irrevocable revoked; he
feels or is dimly aware that *his whole existence is
clouded by falsity.*[17] Nor can the mother or the father
really break away from that bond by going away; their
knowledge of this fundamental bond still binds them to
that trinity of being, although they may deny it over
and over again." [18]

Man, woman, and child are set in a trinity of being
that is irrevocable. And not only throughout our earthly
life but throughout all eternity, it will be true that one
immortal soul knows that through the creative union of
two persons that soul has come into being. This is the
basic human fact that underlies marriage and it is this
fact that should make the marriage union irrevocable.

In his argument for the permanence of marriage,
Brunner points out that in the love of men and women
in contrast to the sexual attraction of the animal world,
there is always the yearning to be alone, the feeling that
the intrusion of a third party is intolerable. He writes,
"For genuine natural love is in its essence monistic.
This does not mean—as modern literature shows us *ad
nauseam*—that the polygamous instinct does not exist,
nor that it is not particularly strong in the male; but it
certainly does mean this: that, quite apart from all ethical obligations, those who love each other do feel the
intrusion of a third person to be intolerably disturbing,
that a strong and genuine love—still quite apart from

---

[16] Italics mine.

[17] Italics mine.

[18] From: *The Divine Imperative*, by Emil Brunner, page 346. By permission of The Macmillan Company, publishers.

any idea of ethical obligation—does want the loved one wholly and solely for itself. Where the emotion of love is genuine and strong, those who love each other know that this bond is permanent. . . . Genuine love is single-minded—indeed that is its power. Genuine love . . . always feels: 'it is with this particular person that I wish to live alone and for always.' " [19]

Paul emphasizes the finality of marriage. He knows that in the self-giving of man and woman to each other there is created a union that is permanent. He knows that marriage is built on fidelity. He knows that underlying marriage there should be a sense of obligation. But Paul also emphasizes the importance of love in marriage. He dares to say that those who are married should love each other as *Christ loved His church*. "Husbands, love your wives, even as Christ also loved the church, and gave himself up for it. . . . Even so ought husbands also to love their own wives as their own bodies. He that loveth his own wife loveth himself: for no man ever hated his own flesh; but nourisheth and cherisheth it, even as Christ also the church . . . Nevertheless do ye also severally love each one his own wife even as himself." [20]

We have seen that Paul affirms in the strongest terms the permanence of the marriage bond. This will lead us inevitably to an examination of the teaching of Paul concerning the dissolution of the marriage bond. Does Paul permit divorce? Does he allow remarriage to those

---

[19] From: *The Divine Imperative*, by Emil Brunner, page 347. By permission of The Macmillan Company, publishers.

[20] Ephesians 5:25, 28, 29, 33.

who have been separated from their former partners by divorce? These and similar questions crowd upon us. The verses in Paul's writing which deal with this subject are limited but are definite and to the point. In the close of the seventh chapter of I Corinthians, Paul says, "A wife is bound for so long time as her husband liveth; but if the husband be dead, she is free to be married to whom she will; only in the Lord." It is clear from this verse that Paul recognizes that the death of either party dissolves the marriage bond. The sexual life of man is part of his whole earthly inheritance. It does not carry over into the life beyond the grave. Even the wedding ceremony contains the words, "until death us do part." In this Paul is in complete agreement with the whole Christian tradition. When one partner to the marriage contract is dead, the other partner is free to marry again.

In verses 10 and 11 of this same chapter, Paul writes, "But unto the married I give charge, yea not I, but the Lord, That the wife depart not from her husband (but should she depart, let her remain unmarried, or else be reconciled to her husband); and that the husband leave not his wife." In this word to the married members of the church at Corinth, Paul feels that he is reproducing the teaching of Jesus. He tells the wife not to depart from her husband and the husband not to leave his wife. But in his parenthesis he does recognize that in some cases a separation may be inevitable. If the separation cannot be avoided, the separation must not be made with a view to remarriage. Probably a majority of the cases of divorce are related to the desire of one partner or the other to marry another person. Paul's instructions would strike at the root of the divorce evil. In commenting on this verse, Goudge says, "The words seem to imply that only for the most serious reasons would a wife be justified in departing. In any case Paul gives no freedom to marry again in her husband's lifetime. Had Paul held that adultery dissolved marriage or made its dissolution permissible, thus leaving either one or both parties free to contract a fresh union, would he not have said so?" [21]

There is, however, one place in which Paul may leave the way to remarriage open. This is found as he is dealing with the problem of a believing wife and an unbelieving husband who deserts her because she has become a Christian. We have seen that although Paul does not advise believers and unbelievers to marry, he does advise the believing woman to remain with her unbelieving husband and the believing man to remain with his unbelieving wife. He has to face, however, the fact that in many cases this will not happen. He knows that some of the women who become Christians will be deserted by their unbelieving husbands. And concerning this situation he writes, "Yet if the unbelieving departeth, let him depart: *the brother or the sister is not under bondage in such cases*." [22] In commenting on this verse, Goudge says, *"let him depart,* i.e. the Christian husband is not to keep his heathen wife by force, nor the Christian wife persistently to intreat her heathen husband to remain with her. *'Is not under bondage.'*

---

[21] From: *Commentary on First Corinthians,* by H. L. Goudge, page 55.
[22] I Corinthians 7:15.

To continue bound to a heathen, who wishes to repudiate the connection would be slavery. Whether St. Paul by these words intends to allow remarriage to the Christian is not quite certain. It is possible that the question is not in his mind. But in any case there can be little doubt that he would have given such liberty, provided that the breach occurred at the time of the conversion and baptism, and not at a later period." [23]

We cannot be dogmatic in our interpretation of this verse, but we can say, on the basis of this seeming exception, that Paul laid firm hold on the Christian understanding of marriage and that he sought to apply it in individual cases with that realism which is always characteristic of him. The Christian ideal of marriage as it is stated in Paul is clear. Its application to all of the concrete situations of life will always be difficult.

The home is the basic institution of society.[24] Within the community of the home, the individual is lifted from a life of isolation and set within a community of life that is based on love. Within the life of the family, the inherent selfishness of man is overcome and man and woman are forced to learn to live for each other and for the children God has given them. Paul moved in the midst of a decaying pagan society. Within that society he built a new society in which marriage was permanent, the life of the home was purified, and the children were given a place in which they could grow into Christian men and women.

---

[23] From: *Commentary on First Corinthians*, by H. L. Goudge, page 56.

[24] Paul deals with the relations of parents and children in Ephesians 6:1, 2; Colossians 3:20; I Timothy 3:4.

CHAPTER VII

The Order of Race—Jew and Gentile

+ +

O NE of the most important of all the questions facing Christianity today is the question of race. Modern inventions have brought the various races of the world into intimate contact with each other. If the Christian church is to be a universal church, it must become a fellowship that transcends race. Is the church to be one and the same among all races, or is the character of the church to be molded by the racial inheritance of every race within which she lives?

The modern world is filled with racial injustice and with racial hatreds. In such a world, can the church build a fellowship in which there are to be found men out of "every nation and of all tribes and peoples and tongues"? [1] Can the church enable men of different races to understand each other and love each other? Can Christianity save the world from race hatred and race wars?

Paul was a Jew. He was born a Jew. He describes himself as a Hebrew of the Hebrews. As a Jew, Paul grew up in the midst of the racial attitudes of that people who above all others have set before the world the phenomena of a racial group that has continued to remain distinct. The Jews were a tribe before they be-

---

[1] Revelation 7:9.

124

came a nation, and after they ceased to be a nation they continued to be a people, a race.

Jewish racial feeling was at bottom religious. The Jews were sure that they were a messianic people, that they were the bearers of a revelation. They knew that they were a chosen people. At times there was a universal outreach in their faith. The prophets and the psalmists are filled with passages in which God passes through Israel to the whole world. But Jewish racial feeling has also at times a tendency to become narrow and selfish. The Jews were tempted to lay their emphasis on the privileges that they inherited as the chosen people. They were apt to forget the responsibility that must always go with privilege.

We must condemn many of the extravagances of Jewish racial feeling. But who can say that the Jews were wrong in their determination to remain a distinct people? The world owes far more to the Jews who refused to be absorbed in the Gentile world than it does to the ten tribes who became lost in the life of Assyria. And if the Jews were to remain a distinct people, who can say that they were wrong in their opposition to intermarriage? The mothers in the homes are always the conservers of the spiritual heritage of the race. A people which intermarries will in time become a people which is absorbed.

Paul was born within the family of Israel. He was born within that portion of Israel in which racial feeling was most intense. He was circumcised the eighth day. He was of the tribe of Benjamin. He was a Hebrew of the Hebrews. As touching the law he was a

Pharisee. The Pharisees were the most patriotic of the Jews. They were the party that stood out against all Greek influences. They were very zealous for the law of Israel. And of himself, Paul could say, "as touching the righteousness which is in the law, found blameless." [2] To the Jewish mob at Jerusalem, Paul can say, "I am a Jew, born in Tarsus of Cilicia, but brought up in this city, at the feet of Gamaliel, instructed according to the strict manner of the law of our fathers, being zealous for God, even as ye all are this day." [3] And in the presence of the council, Paul can declare, "I am a Pharisee, a son of Pharisees." [4]

Paul, far more than most of his contemporaries, understood the basis of Jewish exclusiveness. He says to Agrippa, "And now I stand here to be judged for the hope of the promise made of God unto our fathers; unto which promise our twelve tribes, earnestly serving God night and day, hope to attain." [5] At this time in his life, Paul and the Jews would have differed in their answer as to the way in which the hope of Israel was to be realized. But Paul recognizes that the exclusiveness of Israel is rooted in her consciousness of her destiny. He knows that Israel feels that she cannot lose herself in the nations and continue to be a messianic people, the keeper of the oracles of God. In Romans he asks the question, "What advantage then hath the Jew? or what is the profit of circumcision?" He answers his

---

[2] Philippians 3:5.
[3] Acts 22:3.
[4] Acts 23:6.
[5] Acts 26:6, 7.

own question, "Much every way: first of all, that they were intrusted with the oracles of God." [6]

As a matter of fact, no people ever develop a strong racial consciousness and a narrow racial exclusiveness unless they conceive of themselves as the bearers of something unto the world. This was true of the three great races of Paul's time. The Greeks were the bearers of culture. The Romans were the bearers of law and order. And in our world, the Anglo-Saxon has felt himself to be the bearer of democracy. The Russian has felt that through his people the Marxian ideal for man was being realized in history. The Germans have conceived of themselves as a messianic people with a God-given destiny to rule and to organize Europe. And the Japanese have gone forth to establish a new order in the Orient, an order which most of them believe is for the good of the whole Orient.

The Jews were a messianic people. Their racial exclusiveness was rooted in a messianic consciousness. And young Saul, the Pharisee, stood in the white heat of this messianic consciousness. He believed in the destiny of Israel. He was willing to live and if necessary to die in order that Israel might attain unto the hope of the promise of God made unto the fathers.

At the time of His death, Jesus of Nazareth left the racial exclusiveness of the Jews practically undisturbed. The note of a universal faith was present in Jesus. In the beginning of His ministry, He defied the narrow racial prejudice of Nazareth by reminding the people

---

[6] Romans 3:1, 2.

of the synagogue of the love of God that reached to a widow woman in the land of Sidon and a leper in the land of Syria. We can judge the intensity of Jewish racial feeling by the way in which the people of His own town sought to mob Him because He had dared to express such sentiments.[7] He healed the daughter of the Syrophœnician woman.[8] He found in a Roman centurion a faith He had not found in Israel.[9] He prophesied that many should come from the east and the west and sit down with Abraham and Isaac and Jacob in the kingdom of heaven while the sons of the kingdom were cast out into the outer darkness.[10] And in His resurrection appearances, He instructed His disciples to make disciples of *all* the nations.[11]

But while the universal note was present in Jesus, it was not on this point that He came into irreconcilable conflict with His people. He knew that in the days of His flesh He was sent to the lost sheep of the house of Israel. There is no record of His ever carrying on any extensive ministry to those who were not Jews.[12] He instructed His disciples in their preaching mission not to go into any way of the Gentiles, and not to enter into any city of the Samaritans, but to go rather to the lost sheep of the house of Israel.[13] He knew that the time of the

---

[7] Luke 4:16-30.

[8] Mark 7:26.

[9] Luke 7:9.

[10] Matthew 8:11, 12.

[11] Matthew 28:19.

[12] The conversion of the woman of Samaria and His brief ministry there do not alter this basic fact.

[13] Matthew 10:6, 7; 15:24.

Gentiles had not yet come and He limited Himself to
His mission to Israel. And when His own people rose
against Him and put Him to death, they condemned
Him to die because they refused to acknowledge Him as
the Messiah of Israel. They did not accuse Him of having offered the faith of Israel to the Gentiles.

It was Paul, not Jesus, who came into deadly conflict
with the racial exclusiveness of the Jews. In saying this
we do not mean to set Paul over against Jesus. Paul
knew that he was carrying out his mission as one who
was under the commands of Jesus. The glorified Person who met Paul on the road to Damascus and gave to
him his commission to go to the Gentiles was ONE who
identified Himself by saying, "I am Jesus whom thou
persecutest." [14] It was the risen Christ who appeared to
Paul in the temple and said to him, "Depart: for I will
send thee forth far hence unto the Gentiles." [15] Through
Paul, Jesus Christ entered upon His world mission. But
the man in history who faced Judaism and shook Judaism to its core was Paul.

Saul, the persecutor of the church, probably per-
ceived that Christianity was more than a movement
within Judaism. He persecuted the church for exactly the
same reason that later on the Jews persecuted him. He
saw that in Christianity there was a movement that
struck at the roots of the racial exclusiveness of the
Jews.

It is one of the amazing facts of history that Saul of
Tarsus, the Jew and the Pharisee, should have become

---

[14] Acts 9:5.
[15] Acts 22:21.

Paul the apostle to the Gentiles, the first great apostle of a universal faith. In Paul, the apostle to the Gentiles, Christianity as a universal religion entered into a life-and-death conflict with Jewish nationalism and Jewish racial exclusiveness. An understanding of this struggle is the key to the movement of the book of Acts and the key to the development of the life of Paul.

In the providence of God, the door of faith was opened to the Gentiles by Peter, not Paul. In the early days, Peter was the unquestioned leader of the church. A forward step which aroused such bitter opposition even within the members of the church was much more likely to be accepted if it came through Peter than if it came through Paul. And in the council at Jerusalem it is James who makes the speech which carries the unanimous vote of the council and sets the approval of the church at Jerusalem on the missionary labors of Paul. We mention these obvious facts because it has often been said that in his policy toward the Gentiles Paul stood in opposition to the leaders of the church, especially Peter, the apostle to the circumcision, and James the Just,[16] the head of the church at Jerusalem. Nothing could be farther from the truth. Paul and the apostles stood together over against the Judaizing elements in the church.

But no one can deny that Paul was the man through whom Christianity passed to the Gentile world. Men seldom become alarmed at a theory until that theory becomes incarnate in a fellowship. After the visit of

---

[16] There is some evidence that later on James let himself become the leader of the party of the circumcision. See Acts 21:18 and Galatians 2:12.

Peter to Cornelius, the apostles were quite ready to acknowledge that God had granted to the Gentiles also repentance unto life. But Cornelius and his friends seem to have remained an isolated group. There was no mass movement toward Christianity among the Gentiles of Cæsarea.

It was at Antioch in Syria that unknown Christians began to preach the gospel to Greeks also. These Greeks believed, and there grew up first at Antioch a church in which Jews and Gentiles were received into the faith on equal terms. Paul was associated with the work at Antioch. He went out as a missionary of this church, and when he returned from his first missionary journey, the Gentile church was a reality. Under his preaching churches had grown up in which the centuries-old distinction between Jew and Gentile was broken down. Gentiles and Jews were eating together and were building together a fellowship in which racial lines were being obliterated.

It was at Antioch that Paul faced his first great fight. He faced there Jews from Judea, who taught the Christians at Antioch, saying: "Except ye be circumcised after the custom of Moses, ye cannot be saved." With these men Paul had "no small dissension." The debate was carried on to the council at Jerusalem, and there Paul won a verdict which left him free to go to the Gentile world with the approval of the church at Jerusalem. But his long struggle within the church was only beginning.[17]

---

[17] See Acts 15 for description of this struggle.

Paul went out from Antioch to build all over the Roman Empire churches in which the barriers of race were transcended. He received into his churches Romans, and Greeks, and Jews, and barbarians, and Scythians. He built these heterogeneous elements into a living fellowship which constituted the body of Christ within the Roman Empire. To the end of his life he found himself in conflict with the reactionary elements in the church. The Jewish Christians were never quite sure just what they thought of him. Doubtless there were many of them who went back to Judaism because they did not want to belong to the kind of church Paul was building. The struggle of Paul with the Judaizers revealed in the letter to the Galatians must have been typical of many a bitter battle which he fought. References to a similar struggle at Philippi are found in the third chapter of that epistle.

Paul never ceased to labor to hold together in one church the Jews and the Gentiles. The offerings which he took among the churches of Macedonia and Achaia were part of his effort to bind together the church at Jerusalem and the Gentile churches. And his final trip to Jerusalem had the same motive. The struggle with the Judaizers within the church continued to the end of his life. But the intensity of this struggle probably reached its peak fairly early in the life of Paul. In the closing years of his ministry, he knew that this fight had been won.

But Paul's struggle with Judaism grew in intensity as the years went by. From the time of his conversion on he was hated and feared by the Jews. But as a church composed of both Jews and Gentiles began to grow up within the Roman Empire, an alarmed and aroused Judaism began to see that in the struggle with Paul its very existence was at stake. The Jews were asked by Paul to recognize Jesus as their Messiah and to lose themselves in the larger stream of Christian life, a stream in which both Jews and Gentiles were to meet on equal terms. It is the tragedy of Judaism that, having rejected her Messiah, she also rejected Paul.

The day of Israel's great opportunity was at hand. In the past she had been called to serve God by remaining distinct among the nations. As she was confronted by Paul, she was asked to serve God by losing herself in the larger purpose of God that embraced both Jews and Gentiles in the Christian church. And in the day of her supreme opportunity Israel faltered and shrank back. She did not dare to venture out with Paul to the achievement of her God-given destiny. Thousands of Jews, perhaps hundreds of thousands of them, did follow Paul. These Jews became the core of the Christian church, and in time they were merged in the stream of Christian life. Had the nation as a whole followed Paul, there would have been no Jewish problem in the twentieth century.

But because they knew (and he knew) that the existence of Judaism was at stake, the Jews hated Paul as they hated no one else in the Christian church. They were content to let James go about Jerusalem in comparative security. And when Paul returns to Jerusalem there is little evidence that the church there is experiencing serious persecution. A church can always avoid persecution if it will compromise just a little. But the presence of Paul in Jerusalem was a different matter. Notice the words of James and the elders to Paul when he came to Jerusalem for his last visit. "Thou seest, brother, how many thousands there are among the Jews of them that have believed; and they are all zealous for the law: and they have been informed concerning thee, that thou teachest all the Jews who are among the Gentiles to forsake Moses, telling them not to circumcise their children, neither to walk after the customs." [18] The Jewish Christians were not far wrong in the information they had received concerning Paul. Of course Paul would never have told the Jews to forsake Moses and not to circumcise their children. All he did was to proclaim a message of salvation that had no relation to circumcision or to the keeping of the law of Moses. But that which is rendered unnecessary is soon discarded as useless.

The charge of the Jerusalem mob against Paul was equally true. When the Jews of Asia saw Paul they cried, "Men of Israel, help: This is the man that teacheth all men everywhere against the people, and the law, and this place . . . and hath defiled this holy place." [19] Paul preached a gospel that called upon the Jews to cease to be a separate people. He proclaimed that no man could find salvation by keeping the law. He proclaimed a universal faith that had no vital connection with the temple at Jerusalem. If the Jews had hearkened to him, Judaism would have ceased to exist as a

---

[18] Acts 21:20, 21.
[19] Acts 21:28.

separate movement. The moment in history had come when Judaism was called upon to lose herself in the larger purpose of God. The Jews refused, and because they refused they hated Paul with all the intense hatred that a racial group must always pour out on the head of any man who has called in question the presuppositions upon which its racial exclusiveness rests.

Paul built in the Roman Empire a fellowship in which the divisions of race were transcended. He did more than build this fellowship. He thought out the basis on which such a fellowship must always rest. It was important for him to build the fellowship. His theories would never have shaken the ancient world if he had not incorporated them in a living society. But it was equally important for him to think out the basis upon which such a fellowship must rest. No fellowship can permanently exist in history unless it is undergirded by a system of thought which explains and justifies its existence.

In his speech to the Greeks on Mars Hill, Paul affirms the unity of the human race. He asserts that God "made of one every nation of men to dwell on all the face of the earth, having determined their appointed seasons, and the bounds of their habitation."[20] Science has merely tended to confirm Paul's view of the human race. The race is a biological unity. Between the different races of mankind there may be a vast difference in physical appearance and in cultural attainments, although interbreeding is a biological possibility between

---

[20] Acts 17:26.

all the branches of the human race. But in affirming the unity of the human race, Paul is not thinking so much of its biological unity as of its unity before God. God has made all men. All races are His by creation. God is interested in all men. His redemptive purpose reaches out to all men. All races of men live in the same moral universe and are judged by a God with whom there is no respect of persons. As Paul says in Romans, "tribulation and anguish, upon every soul of man that worketh evil, of the Jew first, and also of the Greek; but glory and honor and peace to every man that worketh good, to the Jew first, and also to the Greek: for there is no respect of persons with God." [21]

But while Paul in his speech on Mars Hill affirms the essential unity of the human race, he does recognize that the unity of the race is a unity within a variety. Of each nation of man it may be said that God has determined "their appointed seasons, and the bounds of their habitation." [22] According to this we can feel that Paul would not object to certain races occupying definite portions of the surface of the earth or discharging a peculiar function in history. But Paul would insist that the church must be one and the same in all these races and that within the fellowship of the church the men of different races should experience a unity that sets them into one vital fellowship.

Paul asserts the unity of all races in Christ. In Galatians, he writes, "For ye are all sons of God, through

---

[21] Romans 2:9-11.
[22] Acts 17:26.

faith, in Christ Jesus. For as many of you as were baptized into Christ did put on Christ. There can be neither
Jew nor Greek . . . for ye all are one man in Christ
Jesus." [23] To the Colossians, Paul writes, "Ye have put
off the old man with his doings, and have put on the
new man, that is being renewed unto knowledge after
the image of him that created him: where there cannot
be Greek and Jew, circumcision and uncircumcision,
barbarian, Scythian, bondman, freeman; but Christ is
all, and in all." [24]

In these verses we get the full sweep of Paul's radical
principle as it is applied to race. In commenting on the
passage in Colossians, Lightfoot says, "To the Jew the
whole world was divided into Jew and Greek, the privileged and unprivileged portions of mankind, religious
prerogative being taken as the line of demarcation. To
the Greek and Roman it was similarly divided into
Greek and barbarian, again the priviliged and unprivileged portion of the human race, civilization and culture now being the criterion of distinction. Thus from
one point of view the Greek is contrasted disadvanta-
geously with the Jew while from the other he is contrasted advantageously with the barbarian. Both distinctions are equally antagonistic to the Spirit of the

---

[23] Galatians 3:26-28.

The complete text of verse 28 is, "There can be neither Jew nor Greek,
there can be neither bond nor free, there can be no male and female; for
ye all are one man in Christ Jesus." I have deliberately dropped out two of
the clauses of the verse in order that we may get the full force of its statement concerning race. But the inclusion of the ineradicable distinction of
sex is important for our interpretation of the verse.

[24] Colossians 3:9-11.

Gospel. The Apostle declares both alike null and void in Christ. . . .

"In this regenerate life, in this spiritual region into which the believer is transferred in Christ, the distinction between Jew and Greek not only does not exist, but it *cannot* exist. It is a mundane distinction, and therefore it has disappeared." [25]

There are two extremes which we must avoid in our attempt to understand these great statements of Paul. Paul affirms that within the sphere of redemption the distinction between Jew and Greek cannot exist. Paul does not mean by this that the Jews who have found Christ have ceased to be Jews and that the Greeks in the church have ceased to be Greeks. He cannot mean this because in Galatians he includes in his sweeping statement the ineradicable distinction of man and woman. Men do not cease to be men because they are in Christ, and women remain women even in the fellowship of redemption. Paul elaborates this idea in his message to the Corinthians: "Only, as the Lord hath distributed to each man, as God hath called each, so let him walk. And so ordain I in all the churches. Was any man called being circumcised? let him not become uncircumcised. Hath any been called in uncircumcision? let him not be circumcised. Circumcision is nothing, and uncircumcision is nothing; but the keeping of the commandments of God. Let each man abide in that calling wherein he was called. . . . Brethren, let each

[25] From: *St. Paul's Epistles to the Colossians and to Philemon,* by Lightfoot, 1916, pages 214 and 215. By permission of The Macmillan Company, publishers.

man, wherein he was called, therein abide with God." [26]

This is part of Paul's conservative principle. It is part of the genius of Christianity through which it moves as a message of personal redemption in the midst of the orders of society. It does not move as a principle of violent revolution. It does not make a frontal attack on the orders of society. It can tolerate them because it knows that at best they belong to the temporary society of a perishing world. But in the very way in which it tolerates them it goes about their destruction. If we may write in the spirit of Paul, we can imagine him saying to a Roman, "You do not have to cease to be a Roman to become a Christian. Join the church, and seek to realize what it means to be a Christian Roman in our world. But remember, being a Roman is nothing, and being a barbarian is nothing. The important thing is the keeping of the commandments of God in that situation in life in which you are called to be a Christian."

On the other hand, we must not make the mistake of losing the great sweep of Paul's principle that in Christ there is neither Greek nor Jew by relegating this principle to the world of heaven in a way that has no bearing on our earthly life. The most arrogant apostle of race prejudice would probably acknowledge that the distinction of white and black drops out in heaven.

When Paul affirms that in Christ there cannot be Jew and Greek, he means to cast upon earth a dynamic principle that is tremendous in its sweep. He means that the church is expected to realize in time a fellow-

---

[26] I Corinthians 7:17-20, 24.

ship that bears witness to that world of eternity in which the distinctions of earth no longer exist. Paul does expect the church to create within our world a fellowship in which the distinctions of earth have become unimportant. He does expect the church to realize within her own fellowship, the unity of mankind, the freedom from racial prejudice that is characteristic of the sons of God. And he expects the church to undermine and ultimately to destroy those pagan attitudes toward race which characterize the life of society as a whole and represent a denial of the Christian conception of the universal brotherhood of man.

The epistle in which Paul attempts most seriously to explain the power of Christianity to break down the barriers between Jew and Gentile is the Epistle to the Ephesians. It is not by accident that this passage is found in the epistle in which Paul presents most clearly his conception of a universal church. The power of Christianity to unite men of different races is closely related to its power to build a world church. This passage is so important that it is necessary for us to quote the whole passage in order that the details of the text may be clearly before us.

"Wherefore remember, that once ye, the Gentiles in the flesh, who are called Uncircumcision by that which is called Circumcision, in the flesh, made by hands; that ye were at that time separate from Christ, alienated from the commonwealth of Israel, and strangers from the covenants of the promise, having no hope and without God in the world. *But now in Christ Jesus ye that once were far off are made nigh in the blood of Christ.*

*For he is our peace, who made both one, and brake
down the middle wall of partition, having abolished in
his flesh the enmity, even the law of commandments
contained in ordinances; that he might create in himself of the two one new man, so making peace; and
might reconcile them both in one body unto God
through the cross, having slain the enmity* thereby: and
he came and preached peace to you that were far off,
and peace to them that were nigh: for through him we
both have our access in one Spirit unto the Father. So
then ye are no more strangers and sojourners, but ye
are fellow-citizens with the saints, and of the household
of God, being built upon the foundation of the apostles
and prophets, Christ Jesus himself being the chief corner stone; in whom each several building, fitly framed
together, groweth into a holy temple in the Lord; in
whom ye also are builded together for a habitation of
God in the Spirit." [27]

Paul boldly says that in Christ Jesus the Jew and the
Gentile who once were afar off are made nigh in the
blood of Christ. He says that Jesus Christ is their peace.
The expression here means that Jesus Christ is the one
who has made peace between Jew and Gentile. Christ
has broken down the wall of partition that separated
Jew and Gentile. How has Christ been able to do this?
Paul answers that He has been able to do this because
He has abolished in His flesh the enmity, even the *law
of commandments* contained in ordinances. In other
words, Paul says that the barrier that stood between

---

[27] Ephesians 2:11-22.

Jew and Greek was the law. It was the law that kept the Jew distinct. It was the law that forbade intermarriage. The law was deliberately designed to keep the Jew distinct. The Jews remained a peculiar people because they exalted the law as a way of salvation. But if it was the law that kept the Jews from being absorbed in the Gentile world, it was the law that kept the Gentiles from becoming Jews. When the Gentiles first began to come into the church, some of the Jewish Christians said unto them, "Except ye be circumcised after the custom of Moses, ye cannot be saved." [28] Paul knew that such a statement was fatal. The Gentiles might be willing to become Christians, but they were not willing to become Jews in order to become Christians. Paul's statement was accurate. The law of commandments contained in ordinances was the impassable barrier that stood between Jew and Gentile.

But Paul states that Jesus has abolished the enmity. He says that through His cross, Jesus Christ has slain the enmity. Through His death on the cross Jesus offered to both Jew and Gentile a new way of salvation. The Gentile was saved by putting his faith in what God had done for him on Calvary. The Jew was saved by putting his faith in what God had done for him on Calvary. Men are not saved by obedience to the law. They are saved by faith in Christ. The law as a way of salvation has been abolished. And because the law as a way of salvation has been abolished, the enmity between Jew and Gentile has been broken down.

---

[28] Acts 15:1.

Through Christ, God has made of Jew and Gentile one new man. He has reconciled them both to God, and in bringing them to God He has brought them to each other. That which Jesus has done for the Jew and the Gentile He can do for men of other races. He can break down the wall of partition between them and create in Himself of the two one new man, so making peace.

But before men of different races can find peace with each other through Jesus Christ, they must all learn to come to Him by the same road, that is, by faith in His atoning death on the cross and by this alone. The Jew wanted to find salvation by faith in Jesus Christ and by obedience to the law of Moses. The Gentile wanted to find salvation by faith in Jesus Christ and by Greek culture. This is the fatal "and" which has destroyed the unity of the church. The church must be the same among all races and among all nations. But we can only have a universal church in a world of nations when the church in each race breaks all entangling alliances with the culture of the race within which she moves and builds her message of salvation on faith in Jesus Christ and on this alone. The church as Paul understands it is built on the apostles and prophets, Jesus Christ Himself being the chief corner stone. If the church in every nation is built on the witness of the prophets and the apostles to Jesus Christ, then the church will be the same in every nation, and Christians all over the world will be able to realize their unity because they will all have been built into *the one new man*.

Christianity in our day is in danger of being shattered into racial and national churches which have little in common save a name, and all too often this common name is used to cover concepts that are mutually exclusive. If Christians are to continue to understand each other in our world, then we must learn that the church in every race and in every nation must be built on the same foundation and Christians everywhere must find salvation through faith in Christ and through this alone.

We have tried, in presenting Paul's teaching concerning race, to present it in general terms, to find our illustrations in the specific problems which he faced, and to work from them to general principles which would be valid for any racial situation in any land. But it would be deeply sinful for the minister of a church which holds its membership in the southern portion of the United States to write a chapter on race in which he did not try to face, on the basis of Paul's thought, the actual racial situation with which the Christian church is confronted in the territory that is covered by the church within which his ministry is carried on.

From this point of view a statement prepared by Ivan Lee Holt is very much to the point. "Each national group is quite ready to give advice on another nation's racial problems. We in America have felt keenly and said much about the treatment of the Jews in Germany. More than one group in America has expressed its opinion of the policy of Great Britain in India. On the other hand, any church assembly in Great Britain can be aroused by the unchristian treatment of Negroes in the United States. Any real solution of race relations requires that each nation face its own problems. Before we in America tell other nations what to do we must confront our own distressing situation." [29]

It is important that each nation and each section of a nation should confront in the name of Christ its own racial situation, because it is only as the word of the church is spoken in the midst of a knowledge of the actual conditions which the church faces that the word of the church becomes a real word that is definitely related to the actual historical situation which the church faces. Here as in other cases an idealism that has in it no note of realism is about as apt to be wrong as a realism that has in it no note of idealism.

In a limited sense there is an analogy between the racial situation of the Jew before the time of Paul and the racial situation of a small white minority when surrounded by the people of other races. The Jews knew that they belonged to a messianic race and that their race would be able to perform its God-given destiny only as it remained distinct among the races of the world. In a much more general sense, it is true that the European races have been the bearers of something to the world. In the spread of European civilization over the whole earth there may have been a divine purpose at work in the world. The great expansion of Christianity in the last two centuries has on the whole been the work of the white races. The impact of Western civilization on the undeveloped peoples of the earth has come through the spread of the white race in the earth.

---

[29] From: *Race Relation Message* (February 13, 1938), prepared by Ivan Lee Holt; adopted by the Federal Council's Executive Committee. By permission of the Federal Council of the Churches of Christ in America.

And the strength of the Anglo-Saxon peoples as a colonizing agency in the world has been found in the way in which in every land to which they have gone they have preserved their own civilization. On the continent of North America, the strength of the English civilization in contrast to that of the French or the Spanish is that the English have seldom intermarried with the native peoples. The English colonists brought their women with them. They came to stay. They built a civilization that was solidly English. They could not have done this if they had freely intermarried with the other races. Women are the conservers of the spiritual values of the race. If the Anglo-Saxon men had intermarried freely with the Indian women of America, they could not have built in America a civilization that was English. We are discussing here not a theory but a *fact* of history. The decision of the white race not to permit intermarriage with other races was its decision to remain white. It represented the refusal of this race to permit itself to be absorbed in a mixed civilization. The practical unanimity with which the white race has always reached this decision when in the presence of the colored races of the earth suggests that there is more at stake than mere racial prejudice.[30] The decision of the white race to remain white has usually represented on the part of the white man the feeling that only by this method could his civilization and his culture be preserved. And the intensity of this feeling on the part of the white man is always in proportion to the acute-

---

[30] The French people have shown a remarkable ability to distinguish between race and culture.

ness of the threat to his civilization that is involved by the presence of other races. It would have been just as intense in Massachusetts as in South Carolina if the people of Massachusetts had been forced to face, as the people of South Carolina did, a situation in which they were outnumbered by the people of another race.[31]

No Christian white man could defend the racial injustice that goes on within the South today, but we must recognize that underlying this injustice there is a decision of a portion of the white race to remain white. Who can say that the Jews were wrong in their refusal to be lost in the Gentile world? To which does the world owe most, the ten tribes that were lost in Assyria or the two tribes that remained distinct in Babylon? And who can say that in the period of history through which we have just passed the Anglo-Saxon races in various portions of the globe have been wrong in their decision not to be absorbed in the native races with whom they have lived? It may be that in the end the Anglo-Saxon races will have best served the undeveloped races of the earth through their decision to preserve their culture by remaining white.

Any understanding of Paul's answer to the race situation in the South must flow out of an understanding of the inner dialectic of his thought in which his word to the actual situation arises from a consideration both of the radical and the conservative principles in his

---

[31] There is no one word that adequately carries my meaning in this portion of my discussion. The word *Anglo-Saxon* is too narrow. The word *white* is too broad. The word *Nordic* is also inadequate and has a connotation at present that is bad.

social message. The radical principle is related to Paul's eschatology, to his knowledge of the unity of all men in Christ. His conservative principle is related to the fact that Christianity is primarily a message of personal redemption and that, as such, it tolerates the orders of society and destroys them from within rather than by becoming a principle of violent revolution and making a frontal attack on the whole basis of society. We must look at the race situation in the South from both of these points of view.

First, we must look at the racial order in the South from our understanding of Paul's conservative principle. The individual who is born in the midst of Southern society finds inevitably that he is confronted by the existing racial situation. This situation is in a limited sense an order of creation. It roots in the differences that exist between the various families of mankind. The racial situation in the South is definitely an order of history. It has come to exist in the form in which it confronts the individual Christian at present through a complicated process of history. Slavery, and the War Between the States, and the period of reconstruction in the South, have all played their part in molding this order of society. No one would claim that the existing situation in the South represents the ultimate will of God for society. No one can deny that it does represent the God-given framework within which the individual Christian must seek to realize the meaning of Christian life.

In this situation we speak in the spirit of Paul when we say that the first word of Paul to the individual

Christian would be to urge him to tolerate the existing situation as an order of history and to seek within it to know and to do the will of God. We can paraphrase the words of Paul as we imagine him saying to men of both races, "Only as God has distributed to each man, as God hath called each, so let him walk. And so I ordain in all the churches. Was any man called being a member of the white race let him not leave his race. Hath any man been called as a member of the black race let him not cease to be a Negro. Being white is nothing and being black is nothing, but the keeping of the commandments of God. Wast thou called being a member of the black race care not for it. Brethren, let each man wherein he was called therein abide with God." [32]

The message of the word of God is preached and a man of the Negro race hears and believes. Through faith in Christ he finds forgiveness of sins and lays hold of the life that is everlasting. He cannot set himself against the whole established social order of which he is a part. As a lone individual he cannot alter the whole framework of his life. His first task is to accept the situation in which he finds himself and within that situation to seek to do the commandments of God.

The gospel is preached. A member of the white race hears and believes. Through faith in Christ he finds forgiveness of sins and lays hold of the life that is everlasting. With an insight born of his Christian experience, he may feel the injustice of the whole racial situa-

---

[32] Based on I Corinthians 7:17-24.

tion. But he cannot at once break from his whole racial inheritance. The framework of his life is determined as he moves in the white race in his community. All that he can do is to seek earnestly to know the will of God for him in his situation and to do it.

And the earthly nature of the whole distinction between white and black is understood as each man remembers that when he finally stands before the judge of all the earth he will not be asked concerning the color of his skin but concerning his readiness to keep the commandments of God in his God-given situation on earth.

But Paul's conservative principle is not as conservative as it sounds in the statement we have given it so far, because Paul concludes his advice with that very profound comment, "Brethren, let each man, wherein he was called, *therein abide with God.*" Each man is told to let God into his life situation. In other words, Paul would say to each man that while accepting for the present his situation in life, his first task is to let Christ live with him in this situation.

It would be utterly amazing what could be done in race relations in the South without altering the fundamental pattern of life at all if white men and black men would let Christ enter their lives and control their attitudes in their life situation. Our first task as Christians as we face the order of society is to seek as far as possible to be Christian in it. For men of both races this would mean that their attitudes to those of the other race should be controlled by purity of life, by honesty and integrity in business, by love, sympathy, and understanding. And in the present social situation in the South it might be easier to abide with God as a member of the Negro race than as a member of the white race. The Negro is less deeply identified with the sinful elements of the existing situation.

Paul's first word, his conservative word, would be to accept the order of society into which we are born and to seek to be Christian in it. But this conservative word of Paul's must never be twisted into the attempt to use Christianity as the bulwark of the *status quo* in the South. Part of the genius of the Christian faith may lie in its power to tolerate the orders of society while in the midst of them it proclaims its message of personal redemption. But Christianity is never identified with the preservation of these orders. *Christianity has utterly no inner interest in the preservation for one race of a privileged position as over against another race.* Christianity is no more identified with the preservation of Anglo-Saxon racial privilege than it was identified with the preservation of slavery. The inner drive of Christianity is always toward the abolishment of all distinctions based on birth or on blood, and toward the building of a society in which the brotherhood of all mankind is realized.

This leads us to Paul's radical principle. Paul would remind us that within the sphere of redemption there is no such thing as privileged and unprivileged races. He said unto his own generation, "Ye . . . have put on the new man, that is being renewed unto knowledge after the image of him that created him: where there cannot be Greek and Jew, circumcision and uncircumcision, barbarian, Scythian . . . but Christ is all, and in all." [33] Paul was quite willing to leave the outer form of the orders of society untouched if he was permitted to build within the fellowship of the church a new society in which the unity of all mankind in Christ was realized. Would he not say to Christians of both races in the South that their first great task in the present situation would be to realize within the life of the church a fellowship in which the chasm was bridged in the unity of both races in Christ?

We touch here the whole problem of racial churches as it exists in the South today. It is doubtful if Paul would ever have agreed to the idea of race churches. The formation of churches along purely racial lines would probably have represented to him a fundamental departure from his conception of the task of the church in society. But in the South today we face not a theory but a fact. In the process of history the races have become segregated into racial churches. And this fact confronts us as an order of society which cannot be altered at once. Perhaps it is best that it should not be. A Christianity that is not vital enough to build churches that bridge effectively the chasms of class within the white race could hardly be expected to build churches that bridged the deeper chasm of race. But just because Christians in the South are divided into racial churches, it is utterly essential that Christians of both races should come together in Christ and realize in Him a unity that goes deeper than the divisions of race.

In seeking to realize such a fellowship, the church

---

[33] Colossians 3:9-11.

must do so on the basis of her own inner life. The message of the gospel is not addressed to man as white or black but to man as man. "And the fellowship of those belonging to the church is not determined by blood, therefore not by race, but by the Holy Spirit and Baptism." [34] The church in the South should not be the last bulwark of the old order. She should be the creator of a new society in which the essential unity of all mankind is realized in Christ. And she should do this on the basis of her right to order her own inner life in harmony with the demands of her Lord.

The basic criticism of the church in the South is not that she has failed to make a frontal attack on the whole racial situation. The church would misunderstand the nature of her task in society if she identified herself with this principle of violent revolution. The basic criticism of the church would be that all too often she has settled herself to live comfortably and complacently with a racial situation which she must feel to be unchristian. The church is not true to her inner life when she has ceased to be in tension with that in her environment which is not Christian. The church is not true to her task in society when she ceases to seek to realize in her own inner life the unity of all men in Christ.

There is no absolute word that can be laid down in advance to define the message of Christianity in a given racial situation. The actual word that the church must speak in any given situation must flow from her knowledge of both the conservative and the radical principles

---

[34] From: *Theological Existence Today,* by Barth, page 52. Published by Hodder & Stoughton, London.

in her message and from her understanding of the actual situation which she faces. Before the church there must be Paul's vision of a Christian society in which man is accepted as man, a society in which the distinction between privileged and unprivileged races has dropped out. At the same time there must be in the life of the church a knowledge of the actual conditions of that world of sinful reality within which the church must live. The agony of the church is that she knows both the ideal and the real and that between the two she must seek to understand the will of God for her. Woe to the church that does not understand something of this agony.

CHAPTER VIII

The Economic Order— Working and Sharing

✦ ✦

EVERY Christian must inevitably adapt himself to the economic order with which he must live. The necessity for some form of economic order roots in an order of creation. Man is created and set within his earthly existence as a being who is dependent on food, shelter, and clothing for the perpetuation of his physical life. The demand for these things is therefore woven into the very warp and woof of our earthly life. It cannot be ignored or denied.

But the particular form of the economic order within which the life of the Christian must be lived is always an order of history. It represents a historical development through which men have sought to meet their economic needs. As such it cannot be clearly separated from the political order through which men seek to establish a stable government. The economic order is always related to the form of the political order within which it functions. Some form of economic order is necessary for the continued existence of man upon the earth. At the same time the economic order will always represent a historical development through which individuals, or groups, or classes, or races have sought to gain a privileged position as compared with the rest of mankind. The economic order will therefore present at any time in history a historical development in which there is found much that is good and much that is evil. Within the economic order, the will of God will be both affirmed and denied. The Christian in society faces no more delicate task than that which is involved when he seeks to understand the will of God for him as he moves within the economic order.

In its initial impact upon the economic order, the message of Paul is essentially conservative. Paul preaches a message of individual redemption. He calls men to surrender to Jesus Christ. He tells them to realize the meaning of the Christian life in their own life situation. His attitude toward the prevailing economic order would be the toleration of its external form as he sought to lead men within the framework of this economic order to live as Christians. There was much that could be said against slavery as it existed within the Roman Empire. But Paul does not tell slaves to rebel against their masters. He tells them instead to be obedient to their masters and to be diligent and faithful in their performance of their duties.[1]

Christianity is not identified with any peculiar form of the economic order. Christianity has lived with slavery, and with feudalism, and with capitalism. The Christian church can live in the midst of any economic order which permits to man the right to worship God according to the dictates of his own conscience and the right to seek to realize the meaning of being a Christian in the midst of society. Christianity could live with Socialism

---

[1] Ephesians 6:5-8; Colossians 3:22-24.

or with Communism. By this we mean that Christianity could continue to exist in the midst of some form of the economic order in which the natural resources of the nation and the tools of production were owned by all and were used for the good of society as a whole rather than for the profit of individuals. The message of Christianity could not fail to come into conflict with any form of Communism which exalts itself into an idolatry and offers itself as a way of salvation for the whole life of man. Christianity in the Western world lives in a society in which the prevailing economic order is capitalism. Christianity tolerates that form of the economic order and seeks to show both owners and workers how they may be Christian within the economic order in which they must live. But Christianity is not identified with the preservation of capitalism as a permanent form of the economic order. When we understand the genius of Christianity, we can realize that the faith which Paul preached might find some form of co-operative society more congenial to its life than the competitive society of modern capitalism.

But the first message of Christianity to the individual is to urge him to seek to be Christian within the economic order which presents to him the framework within which his Christian life must be realized. The individual worker who lives in America cannot alter the form of society before he seeks to live a Christian life. All that he can do is to accept the existing situation as an order of history that presents to him the God-given situation in which he must seek to live as a Christian. And the individual employer of labor will find that he faces a very similar situation. If he is to continue to operate his business, he must adjust himself to an economic order which confronts him as already established. He may find it difficult to live a Christian life in this situation, but this is the situation in which his Christian life must be lived. The final impact of Christianity may completely change the outer form of the economic order, but in its first approach to this problem Christianity assumes the prevailing economic order and speaks its word directly to the man who must live within that order of society.

God has so ordered our earthly life that we cannot continue to live unless we receive day by day our daily bread. In most climates, men need more than food. They must have clothing and shelter. And in the midst of the civilized world, men inevitably find that they are in need of many of the products of the labor of other men. This means that every man must enter the economic order and seek within that order to provide for his own necessities and for the needs of those who are dependent upon him. For most men, this means that in one way or another they must earn the money with which they will buy the things they need. The necessity for making a living is unquestionably a major interest in human life.

Paul does not ignore this fundamental need of human life. He proclaims to all men the necessity and the dignity of work. To the Ephesians, he writes, "Let him that stole steal no more: but rather let him *labor,* working with his hands the thing that is good, that he may have whereof to give to him that hath need." [2] And he writes to the Thessalonians, "But we exhort you, brethren, that ye abound more and more; and that ye study to be quiet, and to do your own business, and to work with your hands, even as we charged you; that ye may walk becomingly toward them that are without, and may have need of nothing." [3]

Paul knows that dishonesty goes with laziness. If men do not earn their living by their own labor, they will be tempted to seek to get the money they need through some form of dishonesty. In a similar vein, Paul tells his converts to work in order that they may have need of nothing. It is through hard work that Paul would have his converts provide for themselves the things that they need. He refuses to let those who will not work become a burden on the charity of the church. It was his custom always to command, "If any will not work, neither let him eat." [4]

Paul knows that those who will not work are the ones who are tempted to *walk disorderly* and to become *busybodies*. He would have approved the old maxim, "Satan finds some mischief still for idle hands to do." One of the tragedies of unemployment in our world is that men need work to keep them busy and to keep them from falling into sin. Paul knows also that Christians will not receive the approval of those outside the faith if they are given to idleness and to laziness.

Paul urges Christians to work in order that they may

---

[2] Ephesians 4:28.
[3] I Thessalonians 4:10-12.
[4] II Thessalonians 3:10.

have something to share with those who are in need. In this way he lifts the work of the Christian above the plane of selfishness. As we create more than we need for ourselves, we are able to share with others who are in need.

Through all of Paul's comments upon the importance of work, there runs an insistence upon the dignity of manual labor. He tells both the Thessalonians and the Ephesians that they must *work with their hands*. He is proud that with the labor of his own hands he has ministered to his necessities.[5] He had been trained in the trade of tentmaking, and at times he supported himself by returning to his trade.

Paul proclaimed the necessity and the dignity of work. He was deeply concerned to so train his converts that the man who became a Christian should become a better workman because he was a Christian. He told the Ephesians that the workers of the world should do their work as unto Christ.[6] What Paul means is that each Christian as he faces the task of the day should realize that the work he must do that day is part of the task that has been given to him by Christ. In this way Paul would lift all service to man to the plane of service to Christ. As Christians we must face the task that lies before us as the work which Christ has given us to do that day. The student in school should consider his lessons as a God-given task. He should feel that in mastering them he is performing the will of God for him.

The farmer or the carpenter should face his daily work

---

[5] Acts 20:34.
[6] Ephesians 6:5-8.

as the way in which he will serve God for that day. Every man should do his work as unto God. There is a kind of service which Paul says is ruled out when the Christian realizes that he must do his work unto God. Christians are to do their work with fear and trembling, in singleness of heart—*"not in the way of eyeservice, as men-pleasers."* [7] There are servants who will not work unless they think their employers are watching them or can check up on them in some way. Their only desire is to do as little work as it is possible to do to hold their jobs. There are men who are interested only in the appearance that their work will make to others. Such an attitude toward work is essentially unchristian. The Christian must conceive of his work as a task that has been set him by his God. He must seek to discharge it in a way that will be well pleasing to God. This conception makes impossible all cheap and shoddy work. It insists that men must do their work "as ever in their great Taskmaster's eye."

The whole moral fiber of a man's living is determined by his attitude toward his work. No man can grow in moral character when he is lazy or indifferent about his work. The child who consistently slights his work will find that he is undermining the whole basis for character. Every man must give an account unto God for the way in which he does his work.

Paul goes deeper than this and says that the Lord who watches the way in which every Christian performs his daily task will see to it that no man loses his reward for

[7] Ephesians 6:6.

work that is conscientiously and faithfully performed. He tells the Colossians to do their work, "as unto the Lord, and not unto men; knowing that from the Lord ye shall receive the recompense of the inheritance: ye serve the Lord Christ. For he that doeth wrong shall receive again for the wrong that he hath done: and there is no respect of persons." [8] He tells the Ephesians to do their work "as unto the Lord, and not unto men: knowing that whatsoever good thing each one doeth, the same shall he receive again from the Lord." [9] Paul says that over all men as they work there stands the Christ. The man who cheats as he does his work may avoid the judgment of men, but the Christ who controls our universe will bring it to pass that the wrong which the man has done will return unto him. And the same Christ will see to it that no faithful service remains ultimately unrewarded.

Surely the employers of labor could not object to their workers having a Christian attitude toward their jobs. There is no place in the life of the Christian for a careless and an indifferent attitude toward work. But Paul's word to the workers is always balanced by his word to the employers of labor. The worker must be Christian in his attitude toward his job and his employer. But the employer must also be Christian in his attitude toward the men who work for him. The masters are to render unto their servants that which is just and equal: knowing that they also have a Master in heaven.[10] No em-

---

[8] Colossians 3:23-25.
[9] Ephesians 6:7, 8.
[10] Colossians 4:1.

ployer of labor who is a Christian can assume an irresponsible attitude toward the welfare of the men who work for him. The worker must do his work as unto Christ. And the employer must remember that he has a Master in heaven. And because the employer also is under Christ, he must render unto his men that which is just and fair. Paul does not go into detail here but we can be sure that, under that which is just and fair, he would include such things as the right of the working man to decent conditions of work, to reasonable hours of labor, to a living wage, and to a fair share of the wealth that is created by his labor. No Christian employer has a right to grow rich while paying a starvation wage to the men who work for him.

The employer of labor today stands in the midst of a competitive economic order. The employer who is a Christian may be forced to compete in the open market with other men who may not be troubled by a Christian conscience. To be a Christian employer of labor may not be easy in our world. But no Christian who buys the labor of other men can avoid his responsibility to God for the way in which he treats the men who work for him.

Paul reminds us that the same God who is Lord of the working man is also Lord of the employer, and that there is no respect of persons with God. The employer and the employee stand in the same moral universe. The employer also cannot escape the fact that if he does wrong he will receive again for the wrong he has done. And the employer who is faithful in his attempt to be a Christian in his life situation is certain to receive his reward from the Lord. Employer and employee stand on equal terms before God. God is just as deeply interested in the soul of the humblest laborer as He is in the soul of the richest employer of labor. In Romans, Paul has proclaimed the truth that God is no respecter of persons to show that Jew and Gentile stand on the same plane before God. He proclaims this truth in Ephesians to show that employer and employee when they face God stand on a plane where there is no distinction between them.

Paul is confident that the task of the church in the economic order is to build a fellowship in which both employers and employees realize their unity in Christ. He can say that in Christ Jesus there is neither bond nor free. He could also say that in Christ Jesus the distinction between the employer and the employee drops out. It is tragic from this point of view that our Protestant churches have in many cases become class churches in which the employers worship in one church and the employees in another. Paul tells the Christian owner, Philemon, to receive the Christian slave, Onesimus, "no longer as a servant, but more than a servant, a brother beloved, specially to me, but how much rather to thee, both in the flesh and in the Lord." [11] Would he not tell every Christian employer to receive every Christian employee as a brother, beloved, in the Lord? Class chasms are widening in our world. The proletariat stand on one side, and the capitalists stand on the other. The two groups have very little in common. It is the task of the

---

[11] Philemon 16.

church to proclaim her message of redemption to both groups and to build both groups into one fellowship in Christ. If the church can do this, she may pave the way for a new understanding between capital and labor and save the world from class war.

As an integral part of Paul's message to the Christian in the economic order, we must consider his teachings concerning the stewardship of wealth. We enter here an important field that is richly developed in Paul's letters. But for the purposes of our study we are interested merely in a brief summary of Paul's teachings in order that we may see their bearing on the life of the Christian in the economic order.

In thanking the Philippians for the money which they have sent to help him with his work in Rome, Paul expresses his gratitude to them for their fellowship in the furtherance of the gospel.[12] In so doing, Paul reminds them that through their giving they have become partners with him in his great task of proclaiming the gospel. As we follow out this line of thought, we can understand that Christians through their giving can become active partners with all those who are engaged in the building of Christ's kingdom. In this way, the money that is controlled by Christians can be set to work in those causes which lie close to the heart of their Master. Most Christians must continue to give the major part of their time to the work which is for them their means of earning a living. But all Christians are able through their giving to become partners in such enter-

---

[12] Philippians 1:5.

prises as Home and Foreign Missions, Christian Education, Sunday School Extension, and all of the other causes that find their place in the work of the church.

One of the absorbing interests of Paul's life was the offering which he sought to raise among the Gentile Christians for the suffering saints at Jerusalem. He refers to this offering in Romans 15:25-27. But when he writes his letters to the Corinthians he is actually engaged in the raising of this offering. In the sixteenth chapter of I Corinthians and in the eighth and ninth chapters of II Corinthians, we find the passages in which Paul makes his appeal for this offering. A study of these chapters will show that Paul expected the church within the Roman Empire to be a great brotherhood in which on a voluntary basis there was a sharing of wealth within the fellowship of the church. He felt that no Christians should live in luxury while their brothers in the faith were lacking in the necessities of life. Paul expected this process of sharing to go on within the local churches. And he envisioned a church in which Christians all over the Empire would be bound together by a sharing of wealth which was to be a visible sign of the reality of the church as a world fellowship. An application of this principle to the world situation today would mean that within the fellowship of the church men should be able to experience a brotherhood that stood between them and the extremes of economic need.

Paul is aware also of the dangers to the souls of men which are to be found in false attitudes toward wealth. He knows that covetousness may become an idolatry in which men put the love of material possessions above their love for Jesus Christ.[13] He knows that those who are rich in this present world may come to put their trust in their riches and that because of this they may find it impossible to attain to a life of dependence upon God.[14] Paul realizes that the possession of riches is apt to lead to a spirit of pride and arrogance which is the very antithesis of the attitude of humility which should characterize the life of the Christian.[15]

Paul knows that the love of money may become a root of every kind of evil.[16] A false attitude toward money is one of the roots of every great social evil. The abuses of the liquor traffic root in the love of money. One of the roots of commercialized prostitution is the passion for money. The love of money lies behind the sin of gambling. Modern wars root in part in economic causes. The desire for money is one of the causes of corruption in politics. The love of money is not the only root of these great social evils. Here as in other cases money is a means to an end. The social evils root ultimately in all of the lusts of men. But a false attitude toward money is unquestionably one of the major roots of the social evils.

Paul knows what the love of money can do to men. He knows that "they that are minded to be rich fall into a temptation and a snare and many foolish and hurtful lusts, such as drown men in destruction and per-

---

[13] Colossians 3:5.
[14] I Timothy 6:17.
[15] I Timothy 6:17.
[16] I Timothy 6:10.

dition." [17] He knows that every man has an immortal soul with its possibilities of an eternal destiny. He has seen men led astray from the faith by their love of money. He feels the terrible tragedy which is involved when mortal men lose their immortal souls because of their love of the material goods of this present world.

For these reasons, Paul reminds men of the narrow limits within which the things that money can buy are able to minister to the life of man. He writes, "For we brought nothing into the world, for neither can we carry anything out." [18] In the thinking of Paul, the period of time that lies between the cradle and the grave is merely the *small moment* in the full life of the child of God. But it is only within this period that material possessions can minister to the life of man. Paul urges men, therefore, to so deal with their material possessions that they may lay "up in store for themselves a good foundation against the time to come, that they may lay hold on the life which is life indeed." [19] He suggests that men can do this by being rich in the good works that they have done with their money during their earthly pilgrimage.[20]

In all of his discussions of Christian stewardship, Paul does not raise at all the question as to the outer form of the economic order. He demands, of course, honesty and justice. He preaches the necessity and the dignity of labor. But he has very little to say concerning the way

---

[17] I Timothy 6:9.
[18] I Timothy 6:7.
[19] I Timothy 6:19.
[20] I Timothy 6:18.

in which the Christians are to earn their money. He assumes that they must enter the prevailing economic order and that through finding their place in this order they will earn their money. But Paul does bring powerful pressure to bear on the conscience of the individual Christian who must determine the way in which he will use the money that is his. In this way he strikes at the weakness of an uncontrolled individualism. Within a capitalistic society the control of large resources does at times pass into the hands of a few individuals. And one of the weaknesses of such a society is that it has no effective social control over the way in which such individuals will spend their money. But Paul does not feel that the individual Christian is free to spend his money as he pleases. The Christian is under Christ and he must give an account of his stewardship to his Lord and Master. A large proportion of the resources of America are administered by those who in name at least are Christian. A major task of the church is that of bringing to bear on the individual Christian conscience the whole conception of Christian stewardship which is found in the New Testament. If Christians in America would administer their wealth in harmony with the advice of Paul, it would bring about changes in our social order which would be deep and far-reaching. Without altering at all the external form of our economic order, we can ameliorate its worst abuses by insisting that Christians shall be Christian in the way they spend their money. And within the message of Paul there is a motivation for this kind of stewardship that cannot be found outside of the Christian faith.

The attitude of Christianity toward the economic order is in the beginning essentially conservative. Paul would tell men to accept the economic order within which they were born as the God-given framework within which they are to seek to live the Christian life. He would tell Christians that so far as possible they should seek to Christianize the existing social order. The evils of capitalism could be ameliorated in many ways if employers and employees would be Christian in their attitude toward their work. But when we have adequately stated the application of Paul's conservative principle with regard to the economic order, we have not spoken the last word of the church with regard to the economic order. We need also to bring to bear on the economic order the full force of the radical principles that are present in the thinking of Paul. And the word of the church at any given moment in history must arise from a knowledge of both the radical and the conservative principles that are present in the Christian message. In our study of the economic order, we must not fail to understand the dialectic nature of all of Paul's social thought.

The economic order as a whole must feel in time the impact of the Christian understanding of God and of man. The economic life of man must be brought into harmony with the ultimate purpose of man in the universe. This means that the autonomy of the economic order must be shattered. The escape of the business world from moral and social controls must be checked. The purpose of the economic order is to produce and to distribute the material goods which men need. And man, the child of God, should be able to regulate the economic order in the interests of all of God's children. Out of the heart of the Christian faith there should arise an effective criticism of those features of the existing economic order which are "making it harder for the generality of men to live Christian lives." [21]

The prevailing economic order of America is capitalism. The abuses of capitalism are evident, and because they see these abuses Christians are apt to forget the blessings that have come through this form of the economic order. The American economic order has developed a capacity to produce that is remarkable. Ultimately a people can enjoy the material goods which it is able to produce. And the only effective way to abolish poverty is to increase the capacity of men to produce. American labor enjoys a standard of living which has never before been attained by the laborers of the world. This high standard of living has been brought about in the midst of a free society in which the basic rights of men have been protected. And American society has shown the capacity to correct the worst of the abuses of the economic order and to move forward without violent revolution toward social gains of major importance.

Any fair analysis of the social situation should recognize the social gains that have been realized in the midst of a capitalistic society. But the knowledge of these gains should not blind us to the abuses that seem to be inherent in capitalism as an economic order. Capitalism

---

[21] The wording here is taken from the Acland Amendment to the Resolutions of the Malvern Conference. See page 173.

has a tendency to treat human labor as a "commodity" just as slavery treated human beings as "chattel." The labor of men and women is a "commodity" but it is much more than a commodity. Capitalism has a tendency to exalt material values over human values. The driving power of capitalism is the profit motive. And when the higher interests of mankind have come into conflict with the demand for dividends, they have gone down with a regularity which is sickening. Capitalism has not brought about an adequate distribution of wealth. In America, we are able to produce wealth. We have an industrial plant and a wealth of mineral and agricultural resources sufficient to give us the material goods necessary for an adequate standard of living for all of our people. But a large proportion of the people continue to remain underfed and inadequately clothed. And capitalism has not been able to guarantee to the worker security of employment. The worker is constantly haunted by the fear of losing his job. And in times of depression the suffering of the laborers through unemployment may be very intense.

A fine example of the criticism of capitalism which can arise from the midst of a Christian community is found in the Acland Amendment to the Resolutions of the Malvern Conference, which reads in part as follows:

"There is no structural organization of society which can guarantee the coming of the Kingdom of God on earth, since all systems can be perverted by the selfishness of man. Therefore the church as such can never commit itself to any proposed change in the structure of society as being in itself a sure means of salvation.

"But the church can point to those features of our existing order which, while they do not prevent individual men and women from becoming Christians, do act as stumbling blocks making it harder for the generality of men to live Christian lives.[22]

"In the present situation we believe the church should declare that the maintenance of that part of the structure of our society by which the ownership of the great resources of our community can be vested in the hands of private individuals, is such a stumbling block. As long as these resources can be so owned, men will strive for their ownership. Those who are most successful in this struggle will have sought this ownership for themselves as individuals and will be regarded as the leaders of our economic life. They will thereby set the tone of our economic life. As a consequence, it will remain impossible to abandon a way of life founded on the supremacy of the economic motive, or to advance nearer to a form of society founded upon a belief in the authority of God's plan for mankind.

"The time has come, therefore, for Christians to proclaim the need for seeking some form of society in which this stumbling block will be removed. Those of us who support this resolution pledge ourselves to do so." [23]

---

[22] Italics mine.

[23] The full text of the Resolutions of the Malvern Conference is published in *The Christian Century* for February 19, 1941, pages 253-255. The Malvern Conference was called by the Archbishop of York in January, 1940, "to consider from the Anglican point of view what are the fundamental facts which are directly relevant to the ordering of the new society that is quite evidently emerging and how Christian thought can be shaped

We do not have to express complete agreement with the Acland Amendment to see in it the approach of the church to the economic order from a point of view that is typically Pauline. The amendment declares that *no structural order of society can guarantee the coming of the kingdom of God. It insists that all systems can be perverted by the selfishness of man* [24] and that the church can never commit itself to any proposed change in the structure of society as being in itself a sure means of salvation.

The amendment makes it clear that men can be Christian within a capitalistic society. Individual men and women can and must seek to be Christian in the situation in which they find themselves. But the amendment asserts that it is the task of the church to point out the features of the existing order which *"act as stumbling blocks making it harder for the generality of men to live Christian lives."* The church must always criticize the features of the existing social order which make it hard for the generality of men to live Christian lives.

With a true understanding of the necessity for historical decision in the actual situation which the church faces, the framer of this amendment declares that the time has come for the church in England to declare that the "maintenance of that part of the structure of our society by which the ownership of the great resources of our community can be vested in the hands of private

---

to play a leading part in the reconstruction when the war is over." The resolutions as a whole were adopted unanimously. The Acland Amendment was presented by Sir Richard Acland, Liberal member of Parliament. It was passed by "a very large majority."

[24] Italics mine.

individuals" is a stumbling block making it harder for the generality of men to live Christian lives.

The framer of this amendment understands also that Christian thought is futile unless it issues in Christian action. He feels that the time has come in England for Christians to proclaim the need for seeking some form of society in which the stumbling block which he has pointed out will be removed.

We cannot debate here the accuracy of Sir Richard Acland's diagnosis of the situation which will confront the church in post-war England. We can say that he has approached his problem from a point of view that is in harmony with the message of Paul and that he understands the genius of Christianity as it moves as a radical force within the economic order.

The defects of capitalism are obvious to all thoughtful students of the social situation. Can these defects be remedied within the capitalistic system? Will it be necessary for men to overthrow the capitalistic form of the economic order and substitute for it some form of co-operative society? Will the movement forward toward a new order of society come about gradually, or will it come by violent revolution? Even if we admit the defects of the capitalistic system, can we be sure that within some other form of society these defects will be remedied? Is it possible that in attempting to get rid of the abuses of capitalism men will fasten on themselves some new form of tyranny that is worse than capitalism at its worst? These and similar questions are before our generation. They are questions which in one way or another our generation must answer.

Paul does not have an answer to questions such as these. He did not face them. And *such questions can never be answered except as they are faced in the light of the actual conditions of history within which they arise.* But against the background of our study of Paul's social thought we can in a limited way define the attitude of the church in the midst of the social struggle of our generation.

We must make it clear that Christianity is not identified with the existing economic order. Paul accepts the existing order of society and urges Christians to seek to realize the Christian life in their God-given situation. But Paul would not be concerned to support either slavery or capitalism. Christianity has no more interest in becoming the bulwark of capitalism than she should have had in preserving slavery, or in becoming the last stronghold of male dominance. Clear thinking here is utterly essential in our generation. In a world in which capitalism is endangered by some other form of the economic order, those who have most to lose by this kind of social revolution are certain to seek to identify Christianity with the form of the economic order in which their privileges are rooted. Such an identification is certain to be false.

Christianity must never be identified with the existing form of the economic order. And the preaching of the church may be responsible for the unrest in society that calls in question the prevailing form of the economic order. The church proclaims the dignity of man. In so doing, she calls in judgment any order that treats human labor purely as a commodity. The church proclaims the brotherhood of man. In so doing, she passes judgment on an economic order that divides men into class groups and engenders hatred between these groups. The church proclaims the *new man* and the inexpressibly new order of the kingdom of God. In so doing, she becomes a ferment in the life of society. Through her preaching, the church sets in the hearts of men a divine unrest that will not be permanently satisfied with any form of the economic order that represents in history a denial of the will of God for man. This is the ultimate radicalism of the great apostle who caught the vision of the new humanity in which there could be neither bond nor free, bourgeois nor proletariat, but all were "one man in Christ Jesus."[25]

---

[25] Galatians 3:28.

CHAPTER IX

The Social Order—Class Divisions

+ +

THE term, social order,[1] is used in two ways. In its larger sense, the expression describes the whole of the organized life of man. In this sense, the economic order and the political order are parts of the social order. But the term, social order, is also used to describe the life of man as it is organized for society, i.e. the various class groups that exist within the life of the community or the nation. It is in this limited sense of the term that we will study in this chapter Paul's message to the Christian in the midst of the social life of man. In a study of Paul's message as a whole, we dare not ignore the bearing of his message on the social distinctions through which the life of man is divided into class groups.

We must recognize at once that no perfectly clear distinction can be made between the class groups of society and the other orders within which the life of man must move. In America, class distinctions are closely related to the economic order. An abundance of money is usually able to open an entrance into society. And an aristocracy of former generations that has lost its wealth will find that over a long period of time culture and social prestige cannot be maintained without financial resources.

---

[1] The word, *society*, is also used in these two senses.

Class divisions cannot be completely separated from the political order. Usually the class that is in power seeks to rule in its own interests. Any great uprising of the underprivileged classes is certain to have a political as well as a social aspect. In fact, in the Marxian sense of the term the class war is interpreted largely in terms of economics and politics. The proletariat are the workers who do not own their tools. The bourgeois are the middle-class group who control the instruments of production and exploit the workers. The nobility may be grouped with this class or they may be set apart as an aristocracy of landowners. Such distinctions are more economic than social. But we have already discussed the economic order, and as in a later chapter we will discuss the political order our main concern in this chapter is with those social distinctions which, regardless of their cause, divide men in America into class groups.

Social distinctions are also related to educational advantages. The doors of society open more readily to those who are engaged in the professions that require a long period of educational preparation. The doctor, the lawyer, the minister, and the educator will find that through success in their professions they have in part prepared the way for their entrance into society.

Class distinctions are not free from racial prejudice. In many sections, people are called upon to face the closed doors of society purely on the basis of race. This very important aspect of our subject has been dealt with in another chapter and cannot be reconsidered here. But class divisions are never entirely racial. The members of the Negro race in almost any Southern town will be divided into clearly defined class groups that very definitely affect the church life of the Negroes of that town. And in the same town, the chasm between the "planter aristocracy" and the "poor white" may be so deep as to render it very difficult to build both groups into one Christian fellowship.

No one can deny that class distinctions exist throughout the whole of American society. In contrast to the society of other countries, the class divisions of American society are less clearly marked. Individuals pass more freely from one group to another in America than in Europe or in Asia. American society does not face a system of caste which is as fixed as that of India. But even in democratic America one of the most difficult problems faced by the average Protestant pastor is the problem of proclaiming the message of the gospel in the midst of the social distinctions of a community. A consideration of this problem is therefore very relevant to the life of the church in America.

When we turn from a statement of our problem to a study of the message of Paul to man in the midst of society, we realize at once that Christianity is in radical tension with any system of class divisions based on birth or on inherited wealth. Peter opens his speech at Caesarea by saying, "Unto me hath God showed that I should not call any man common or unclean." [2] This was the radical insight in obedience to which Christianity began to move as a healing power in the midst

[2] Acts 10:28.

of the class divisions of the Roman Empire. In the same speech, Peter says, "Of a truth I perceive that God is no respecter of persons: but in every nation he that feareth him, and worketh righteousness, is acceptable to him." [3] And in justifying his action to the apostles at Jerusalem, he says, "And the Spirit bade me go with them, making no distinction." [4] The belief in the equality of all men before God is at the heart of the expanding Christianity in the first century.

This insight into the equality of all men before God which lay at the beginning of an expanding Christianity is constantly reaffirmed and developed in the thought of Paul. In at least three different places, Paul proclaims the truth that God is no respecter of persons. He applies this truth to divisions of society based on religious privilege, economic privilege, or cultural privilege.[5] He would have applied the same principle to the class distinctions of American society.

As an illustration of the way in which the apostles condemned the carrying of class distinctions into the fellowship of the church, we should also notice a passage from James. "My brethren, hold not the faith of our Lord Jesus Christ, the Lord of glory, with respect of persons. For if there come into your synagogue a man with a gold ring, in fine clothing, and there come in also a poor man in vile clothing; and ye have regard to

---

[3] Acts 10:34, 35.

[4] Acts 11:12. In their setting these statements of Peter apply primarily to the problem of distinctions between Jew and Gentile, but no one would deny that they apply with equal force to class distinctions within the same racial group.

[5] Romans 2:11; Ephesians 6:9; Colossians 3:25.

him that weareth the fine clothing, and say, Sit thou here in a good place; and ye say to the poor man, Stand thou there, or sit under my footstool; do ye not make distinctions among yourselves, and become judges with evil thoughts? Hearken, my beloved brethren; did not God choose them that are poor as to the world to be rich in faith, and heirs of the kingdom which he promised to them that love him? But ye have dishonored the poor man. Do not the rich oppress you, and themselves drag you before the judgment-seats? Do not they blaspheme the honorable name by which ye are called? Howbeit if ye fulfil the royal law, according to the scripture, Thou shalt love thy neighbor as thyself, ye do well: but if ye have respect of persons, ye commit sin, being convicted by the law as transgressors." [6]

This description from James of a scene in a gathering of the early Christians shows us that in actual experience the early Christians did not always realize a society in which there was no respect of persons. But the story also shows us that the apostles felt it necessary to rebuke strongly the sin of respect of persons when they saw it in the life of the church.

In a similar vein, Jude condemns Christians who show respect of persons for the sake of advantage.[7] A sinister aspect of the whole class struggle is that for the sake of advantage Christians are tempted to show respect of persons and not to treat all men as equals before God.

Paul, Peter, James, and Jude all agree in applying the

[6] James 2:1-9.
[7] Jude 1:16.

Christian principle that there is no respect of persons with God to all attempts to perpetuate class divisions within the church. But Paul wrestles with this problem in greater detail than the other apostles. In the fourth chapter of I Corinthians, he strikes at the tendency of some of the Corinthian Christians to feel that they are better than others in the church. "Now these things, brethren, I have in a figure transferred to myself and Apollos for your sakes . . . that no one of you be puffed up for the one against the other. For who maketh thee to differ? and what hast thou that thou didst not receive? but if thou didst receive it, why dost thou glory as if thou hadst not received it?" [8]

This passage is directed in part at the pride of man, at the pride of Christian man as he forgets the complete dependence of his life on God. In this the Corinthians are contrasted with the apostles. But the passage bears with equal force on all those tendencies of one group to exalt itself over another group because of the accident of birth. If we may paraphrase his thought, Paul would say to Christians today, "Suppose you were born within one of the first families of the land. What did you have to do with the conditions under which you were born? This is part of the God-given framework within which your life is set. The privileges of your birth do not give you any right on this basis alone to be *puffed up* against your neighbor. If by accident of your birth you have received large opportunities, you must also face the fact that every opportunity carries with it a corresponding responsibility."

---

[8] I Corinthians 4:6, 7.

In a similar manner, Paul would speak of the differences in ability that inevitably differentiate men. There are men of one talent, and of five talents, and of ten talents. There are men of large mental ability. There are others who are born with slow or feeble minds. But Paul would say to the brilliant student, "Who made you to differ from the stupid pupil who sits next to you? It is God who gave you your ten-talent brain. You are all stewards of the talents God has given you, and the one requirement of every steward is that a man be found faithful." Very often the one-talent man renders a truer stewardship of his abilities than the ten-talent man. But in no case is there anything here which should enable one man to exalt himself over another.

The same line of reasoning would apply to those who by "the accident of birth" have inherited wealth. The man who is rich does have a power over his fellow man. But this power must always carry with it a sense of responsibility. To all Christians who are tempted to be puffed up, Paul would ask the questions, "Who maketh thee to differ? and what hast thou that thou didst not receive? but if thou didst receive it, why dost thou glory as if thou hadst not received it?" [9]

We are not to think that the writers of the New Testament would have any man despise his birthright. Both in the Old Testament and in the New, Esau is condemned because he despised his birthright.[10] Every man of honor desires to hand on to his children a name that is free from stain and a family tradition that need

---

[9] I Corinthians 4:7.
[10] Genesis 25:34; Hebrews 12:16, 17.

not be despised. The privileges that come to each individual as the accident of birth have not come by accident alone. Those who are born in the United States of America receive a heritage of political and religious freedom that has come to them through the blood and the toil of their ancestors who in former generations have dared to sacrifice everything that their children might remain free. And if the individual in a community receives as his heritage a noble name and a place of economic and social privilege in the life of the community, it may be that his parents and his grandparents have sacrificed to give him his heritage. There could be no greater folly than that of despising our birthright. The world has no patience with the Esaus who (because in their inner souls they are profane) are willing to sell their birthrights for a mess of pottage. Each generation must seek to pass on to the next generation the accumulated spiritual and cultural values that have been wrought out in the agony of the race. Every individual should respect the heritage which he receives by the accident of birth.

But no man on the basis of his birthright is justified in a pride that has no relation to what he is or to what he himself has done in the world. Each man's responsibility to God and to his fellow man is in proportion to "that which he has received." And of each man in the God-given situation in which he finds himself it is required that he be faithful to his stewardship of the "talents" he has received. There is nothing in the accident of birth that gives to any social group the right to exalt itself over other groups in the community.

We must face the full force of the message of Pauline Christianity as this message calls in question the social divisions of a community. But when we have faced this message fearlessly, we should also realize that it is not in harmony with the genius of Christianity for it to enter a community as a radical and revolutionary force which demands at once the abolition of all class distinctions within the community. Christianity enters the social order not as dynamite but as leaven. It moves quietly within the accepted framework of society. Christianity attacks the pride of class and the arrogance of wealth and the degradation of poverty, but it should not in the beginning ignore the things that in the past have forced the life of a community to organize itself into definite social groups.

In most cases, the class distinctions of a community are based on something that goes much deeper than the accident of birth. The class distinctions of a community usually have in them a moral and spiritual element which Christianity should not ignore. When certain families in a community have drawn together into a social group and have sought to exclude from the intimacy of their fellowship other families in the community, it may be that in the beginning this grouping has taken place as a protest against the breakdown of moral standards and as an effort to preserve within the community a social group in which the standards of conduct were pitched on a plane above the level of the community as a whole. Every society inevitably protects itself by casting out those who flagrantly violate the ethical standards upon which respectable society is based. And in such a situation the task of Christianity is to change men before it attempts to radically alter the social organization of the community.

We may deplore the mistakes and the injustices that are often made as society casts out those who refuse to meet its moral standards. But we cannot fail to recognize that this process as a whole is an aid to morality. Those who have lived in a land where there is no social pressure that undergirds the demands for righteousness know that every man at times needs to be supported by social standards that he cannot violate with impunity.

Paul recognizes that a Christian society must protect itself by casting out of its fellowship those who violate the Christian conscience in an outrageous manner. His treatment of this problem is found in the fifth chapter of First Corinthians. Within the Christian community, a man was living with his father's wife. We are not told the details of the case but the natural explanation would be to assume that his father had married twice. In this case, the man would have been living with his father's second wife. As there is no reference to the woman, we can assume that she was not a member of the Christian community. And regardless of the accuracy of our understanding of the man's offense, we can be sure that his conduct was morally outrageous and that it was generally known. The church in Corinth had acquiesced in the man's conduct and he was still received in good standing in the Christian community. This is the situation that calls forth the wrath of the apostle.

Paul instructs the church at Corinth to put away this

wicked man from their midst. He does this because he knows that evil that is openly tolerated within the Christian community will spread quietly until like leaven it permeates the whole lump. This advice of Paul's is not merely his instruction in this particular case. It represents a principle of action that is to guide the church in all similar cases. He says, "I wrote unto you in my epistle to have no company with fornicators . . . but now I write unto you not to keep company, if any man that is named a brother be a fornicator, or covetous, or an idolater, or a reviler, or a drunkard, or an extortioner; with such a one no, not to eat." [11]

Paul insists that the Christian community should protect itself by casting out of its inner fellowship those who by their sinful conduct reveal that they are living wicked lives. He does not mean that Christians should break off all intercourse with such people. He does mean that they should not be received into an honored place in the Christian brotherhood.

Paul does not comment on the way in which this casting out is to be accomplished. In the days of church discipline, church sessions called offenders before them and suspended them from the Communion or in extreme cases cut them off entirely from the fellowship of the church. The time may come when the church will have to return to this kind of discipline. But in actual practice church discipline proved very difficult to exercise. It could not be exercised at all unless it was practiced consistently. And in many cases information that

---

[11] I Corinthians 5:9, 11. (A. S. V. margin.)

was generally known could not be established in a church court.

Actual cases of the administration of church discipline by the church courts are rare today. There does go on in the church another process which is often equally effective. When a member of a church has done something which outrages the Christian conscience of a community, the people of the church instinctively separate themselves from the person who has violated the accepted standards of Christian society. We have a description of this process in the words of Paul. The Christian people refuse "to keep company . . . with such a one." This kind of excommunication goes on in every community. At times it is unfair. It may be based on false information or on prejudice. But on the whole the process is wholesome. The people of the community know more about each other than the church session is apt to know. And the decisions of a Christian community are usually sound. Through this process the society of the church is protected from condoning evil and permitting evil to spread through the whole fellowship of the church.

And the person who is punished in this way is made to realize that the sin of his life reveals his unfitness to enter the kingdom of God. The fellowship of the church is not based on birth, or wealth, or culture. But the fellowship of the church must be based on faith and on life. The church cannot receive into the intimacy of her fellowship those who are not spiritually prepared to enter.

This process of excommunication by the outraged

Christian conscience of the church needs to be limited in two ways. It needs to be guarded against all Pharisaic self-righteousness. The line of demarcation here is not clear. Very often those within the church may be just as bad in their way as those who are not within the Christian fellowship of the community. But the danger of abuses in the action of the church should not blind us to the simple fact that the people of a community have a right to insist that the condition of being received in the fellowship of the church is a faith in Christ that issues in righteous living. In the second place, this process needs to be carefully guarded against the closing of the doors of the church to those who wish to return by the road of repentance and renewed faith. Sometimes it is easier to bring men back to Christ than it is to bring them back into the fellowship of His church. Paul wrote the Corinthians to put away the wicked man from among them. But he also wrote the Galatians, "Brethren, even if a man be overtaken in any trespass, ye who are spiritual, restore such a one in a spirit of gentleness; looking to thyself, lest thou also be tempted. Bear ye one another's burdens, and so fulfill the law of Christ." [12] And he could remind the Corinthians that many of those who at present stood within the church had at one time been guilty of the worst of sins.[13]

When we say that a church has a right to cast out of its fellowship those who violate its accepted standards of Christian conduct, we are dealing with a matter that is very essential to an understanding of the problem of

[12] Galatians 6:1, 2.
[13] I Corinthians 6:9-11.

class distinctions within a church. There is no place in the church for social exclusiveness based on family standing, or wealth, or natural ability, or educational privilege. But there is a spiritual prerequisite for those who would enter the intimacy of the fellowship of the church, and at this point the church must not lower her demands.

Very often when bitter criticism is directed at the exclusiveness of a church fellowship, this demand is ignored. All too often individuals and families wish to use the church as a stepping stone to security of social position without at the same time being willing to make the surrender of life to Christ that is the source of all genuine Christian experience. We need not be surprised that in the end such people meet with closed doors. The community will not open to them because it knows they cannot be trusted.

On the other hand, the people of a community are usually ready to receive into the full fellowship of the church those who are spiritually prepared to enter. The doors will open to any family when the people of the community are satisfied that the members of this home belong to the fellowship of those who have been cleansed, and justified, and sanctified in the name of the Lord Jesus Christ, and in the Spirit of our God.[14]

Christianity should be a healing power in the midst of the class distinctions of a community. It does not attempt to completely eradicate these distinctions until it has prepared the way by eradicating the conditions

---

[14] I Corinthians 6:11.

that called them forth. But Christianity does seek to build within the community a fellowship that is open to all those who are ready to receive Jesus Christ as their Saviour and live within the community a life that reveals His saving power.

We ought not to discuss this vital subject without attempting to apply the principles we have set forth to the realities of the situation in America. Protestantism in America has a tendency to run to class churches. The denominational divisions originate in part in the social strata. In the cities, we have made very little effort to assign the people of a geographical area to one church. Almost inevitably, the people who are "comfortable together" gather in church groups that are drawn in the main from one section of the population. Some denominations have their membership in the main among the older groups of society. But even when the same denomination has several churches in a town, these churches are apt to differ in the social group from which they draw their main support.

This process is natural and to some degree inevitable. People do not permanently worship in a church unless they come to feel at home in its fellowship, and people naturally feel at home more easily with those who are on something of a par with them in educational opportunity, financial standing, and cultural background. But while this process is to some extent inevitable, it is greatly to be deplored. The easy accommodation of Protestantism to a system of class churches is tragic.

The church would show infinitely more spiritual vitality if it demonstrated its ability to build into one fellowship those from all classes of society who are willing to give themselves in faith and love to Jesus Christ. It was Paul's hope that in Christ Jesus Philemon, the master, and Onesimus, the slave, would experience a fellowship that would make them brothers. And today we must not lose the vision of a church in which the rich and the poor, the privileged and the underprivileged, the educated and the uneducated, can experience a Christian fellowship which makes them one man in Christ. In every true church, there should be a place for any man who is a genuine Christian.

The church that definitely chooses to become a class church may in time disappear. The upper classes usually do not reproduce themselves. They may have a wealth of material resources but they have a poverty of children. In many of the small towns of the South, there are dying churches. They are not dying because all of the people have moved away from the community. The community as a whole may be as populous as ever. These churches are dying because in the past they chose to draw their membership from one social group. Such churches never seriously directed their message to the whole community. They never realized a fellowship that was vital enough to draw believers of all groups into one fellowship. And as the class group from which the church drew its membership died or moved away, the church was left without members and without power in the life of the community.

But while this is a description of some churches it is not a description of all churches. In many cases, the people of the church have expanded their vision of the task of the church in the community and have moved forward to the building of a fellowship which reaches the whole community. May the example of these churches be prophetic? May Christ give to the Protestant churches of America the capacity to cease to be class churches and to seek to minister to the whole of the population in the area for which they are responsible?

We close this discussion of Christianity and class divisions with a quotation from Nicholas Berdyaev. "Every man is made in the image of God, however indistinct that image may become, and every man is called to eternal life; in the face of these truths, all differentiation by class, all political passion, all the superfluities that social life piles daily on the human soul are trivial and unavailing. That is why the problem of the class war, important as it is economically, juridically, and technically, is above all a spiritual and moral problem, involving a new attitude of Christians toward man and society and a religious renewal of all mankind." [15]

---

[15] From: *Christianity and Class War,* by Nicholas Berdyaev, page 123. By permission of Sheed & Ward, publishers.

CHAPTER X

The Political Order—The State

+ +

Paul was a Jew. At the same time, he was a Roman citizen. He was born a citizen of the great empire that for many centuries governed the Mediterranean basin which to Paul constituted the inhabited world. At various times in his life, Paul appealed to his privileges as a Roman citizen. Of the magistrates at Philippi, he could say, "They have beaten us publicly, uncondemned, men that are Romans, and have cast us into prison; and do they now cast us out privily? nay verily; but let them come themselves and bring us out." [1] And we are told that when the magistrates heard that these men were Romans they were afraid and that they came and begged them to go away from the city. When the chief captain at Jerusalem ordered Paul to be examined by scourging, Paul asked, "Is it lawful for you to scourge a man that is a Roman, and uncondemned?" [2] And we are told that the chief captain also was afraid when he knew that he was a Roman, and because he had bound him. [3] When the Jews at Corinth seized Paul and brought him before the judgment seat, the Roman pro-consul, Gallio, saved Paul from their hands and drove the Jews

---

[1] Acts 16:37.
[2] Acts 22:25.
[3] Acts 22:29.

from the judgment hall.[4] A few years later, the town clerk quieted the mob raised against Paul at Ephesus by Demetrius and his fellow craftsmen.[5] During the final trip to Jerusalem, Paul was seized by the Jerusalem mob. The mob intended to stone him, but the chief captain of the Jerusalem band, Claudius Lysias, saved Paul by a swift attack on the mob.[6] And when Paul despaired of receiving justice before the Roman court at Caesarea, he was able to exercise the right of a Roman citizen to appeal his case to Caesar.[7]

Out of the experience of his life, Paul knew the value of the state as the preserver of law and order. The ordered life of civilized man cannot continue to function without the protection of some form of government. We can understand, therefore, that Paul is writing out of a true understanding of the needs of mankind when he declares in Romans that the political order roots in God. He writes, "Let every soul be in subjection to the higher powers: for there is no power but of God; and the powers that be are ordained of God. Therefore he that resisteth the power, withstandeth the ordinance of God: and they that withstand shall receive to themselves judgment. For rulers are not a terror to the good work, but to the evil. And wouldest thou have no fear of the power? do that which is good, and thou shalt have praise from the same: for he is a minister of God to thee for good. But if thou do that which is evil, be

---

[4] Acts 18:12-17.
[5] Acts 19:35-41.
[6] Acts 21:27-36.
[7] Acts 25:6-12.

afraid; for he beareth not the sword in vain: for he is a minister of God, an avenger for wrath to him that doeth evil. Wherefore ye must needs be in subjection, not only because of the wrath, but also for conscience' sake. For for this cause ye pay tribute also; for they are ministers of God's service, attending continually upon this very thing. Render to all their dues: tribute to whom tribute is due; custom to whom custom; fear to whom fear; honor to whom honor." [8]

In addition to the passage from Romans, Paul refers to the civil power when he writes to Timothy, "I exhort therefore, first of all, that supplications, prayers, intercessions, thanksgivings, be made for all men; for kings and all that are in high place; that we may lead a tranquil and quiet life in all godliness and gravity. This is good and acceptable in the sight of God our Saviour." [9] He tells Titus to instruct the Christians to "be in subjection to rulers, to authorities, to be obedient, to be ready unto every good work." [10]

The general trend of all these passages is thoroughly conservative in the advice that is given to Christians concerning their attitude to the state. Christians are encouraged to recognize the state as an order of history, as part of the God-given framework within which their lives are to be lived. As Paul says, "There is no power but of God; and the powers that be are ordained of God." We know enough of Paul's thought to understand that Paul does not deify any political order. But

---

[8] Romans 13:1-7.
[9] I Timothy 2:1-3.
[10] Titus 3:1.

Paul does recognize that the Roman state has come to its place of world dominance by a process of history that is in a sense willed of God. The Roman state exists in history because God has willed that it should exist. The Roman state confronts the Christian of the first century as an abiding political order through which the world in which the Christian must live is governed.

Paul urges on all Christians the virtue of obedience to the government under which they live. Citizens are to obey the laws of the land. They are to respect and obey the officers of the law. Paul says that Christians are to keep the law of the land not only as a matter of wrath but also as a matter of conscience. Some men keep the law because of their fear of the punishment that will follow if they break the law. Christians, of course, will fear the punishment that is meted out to the breakers of the law. But entirely apart from the fear of punishment, Christians are to keep the law because they know it is the right thing to do.

Peter says that Christians are to keep every ordinance of man for "the Lord's sake." [11] Paul says that the ruler is a minister of God. There is a double thought here. Peter probably has in mind the effect on the propagation of the gospel of the obedience of Christians to the law. He feels that as Christians subject themselves to every ordinance of man for "the Lord's sake" they will silence criticism and prepare men for the message of the gospel. But Paul and Peter both go deeper than this in their thinking. They feel that Christians must obey

[11] I Peter 2:13.

the ruler because disobedience to the ruler is disobedience to God. They feel that ordered government is part
of the will of God for the life of man. The ruler is the
representative of a political order that exists through the
will of God. For this reason they feel that disobedience
to him is a sinful rebellion against God's will for society.

We can carry this thought too far. There are very
definite limitations on the responsibility of the Christian to obey the magistrate. But the general principle
of the recognition of the God-given nature of the civil
power is sound. The judge interprets a law that grounds
in justice. The policeman stands for law and for order
in the life of the community. The officers of the political order are the representatives of an order of society
that is ordained of God.

As a particular part of their obedience to the state,
Paul insists that Christians shall be faithful in their pay-
ment of taxes. Tribute is the tax paid by a conquered
nation to the conquering government. The Jews re-
belled against the idea of paying tribute to Rome. "Custom" is the tax that any citizen would have to pay for
the support of the civil government. The Greek word
that is translated "fear" describes the respectful awe that
is felt for one who has power in his hands. The word
translated "honor" describes the reverence that is paid
to a ruler. The Christian is to pay his taxes and to render to the officers of the law the respect and honor
which are their due.

All of this advice is thoroughly conservative. If Paul's
converts heeded his advice, they were good citizens of
the Roman Empire. Their Christianity did not set them

in rebellion against Rome. Through their new faith they gained new reasons for obedience to the power of the state.

Paul's advice to the Christians is combined with a definite understanding of the purpose of the state. In Paul's thought, the officer of the state is "a minister of God to thee for good." The same officer is "a minister of God, an avenger for wrath to him that doeth evil." The state exists for a good purpose. This purpose may be expressed both in a positive and in a negative way. The services of the state are for the good of the community as a whole. The Roman Empire preserved the law and order that were necessary for the development of commerce or for the propagation of the gospel. The Roman state established a system of coinage, built roads, and in many ways served the Empire as a whole. Within the modern state, these services have been greatly extended. The state carries the mail, conducts schools, regulates commerce, administers relief, and in many other ways seeks to serve the nation as a whole.

The power of the just state is used to hold in check the evil of individuals. Those who have lived in a bandit-infested country can appreciate the comparative security of life where the power of an ordered government is established. In many communities the power of government to hold in check the evildoer operates so silently and so smoothly that it is hardly recognized. It is assumed as men assume the atmosphere which they breathe. But if the power of the government is broken and anarchy ensues, men will be able to appreciate to the full the services of a just and stable government.

Paul gives to the state the right to bear the sword. In verse 4, he writes, "for he is a minister of God to thee for good. But if thou do that which is evil, be afraid; *for he beareth not the sword in vain:* for he is a minister of God, an avenger for wrath to him that doeth evil." [12] The magistrate does not bear the sword for display. He bears the sword, and, if necessary, he must *use* the sword. " 'The sword' is the symbol of the executive and criminal jurisdiction of a magistrate, and is therefore used of the power of punishing inherent in government." [13]

Paul recognizes the legitimate use of the police force, the right of the state to inflict punishment on the evildoer—the right of the state, if necessary, to kill. The policeman who shoots to kill to protect his own life or the life of the citizen may be a minister of God doing his duty for the good of the community as a whole. To the state there is given the power to punish men, to place men in prison, and if necessary to kill men. The position of Paul is verified in history. In spite of all idealistic theories to the contrary, no state has ever been able to function efficiently and permanently without the use of the police power.

Does the placing of the sword in the hand of the civil magistrate grant to the state the power to make war? This question comes to us with peculiar force as we live in a world in which nation is rising up against nation and total war threatens to envelop the globe. Is it ever

---

[12] Romans 13:4.

[13] From: *Commentary on Romans,* by Sanday and Headlam, page 367. By permission of Charles Scribner's Sons, publishers.

right for one state to use force against another state? Is the making of war always wrong? Or do situations arise in which the state should call its citizens to arms? Should aggression and tyranny be met with passive resistance? Has the president of a great nation the right to call for the use of force, "for force without stint or limit," in order that the world may be made safe for democracy? What should be the attitude of the Christian toward war? Questions such as these are being asked by Christians today. If Paul has an answer to such questions, it must be along the line of the right of the state to use the police power to maintain order, to protect the life and property of its citizens. There is no other place in the writings of Paul in which this issue is raised.

The distinction between the police power and the war power is obvious. In theory at least, the police power is always a disinterested force that is exercised only at the command of a court of justice. If two individuals have a disagreement and fight it out, the appeal is to force alone. The outcome of the struggle does not decide which man is right. The appeal in such a struggle is to might rather than to right.

Two men have a disagreement. Instead of fighting each other they take their disagreement to a judge. The judge makes a disinterested examination of the case and gives his decision in favor of the man whom he decides to be right. The probability is that force will never be used at all. But if the man who has lost the case refuses to accept the decision, the judge can order the officer of the law to use force if necessary to see that the decision is carried out. Force, if it is used at all, is used by a disinterested party in the name of righteousness. And if force is used, it will be used against the criminal alone and not against innocent members of society. The size of the police force of New York City does not constitute a threat to the security of the citizens of Chicago.

When two nations go to war the appeal is to might rather than to right. And the outcome of the war reveals the strength of the armed forces of the two nations. Justice does not always rest with the winning nation. A world in which nations must settle their differences by an appeal to arms is a world in which might is exalted above right. A world in which every nation does that which is right in its own eyes is a world of international anarchy.

But when we think more deeply into the problem, we can see that the analogy between the use of the police power and the use of the war power is closer than it appears at our first glance at the subject. In the last analysis, the sword is placed in the hand of the magistrate because men know that an ordered society cannot exist in a world in which every powerful and unprincipled man is permitted to do that which is right in his own eyes. Behind the policeman there lies the will of society that ordered government shall be maintained. The sword is placed in his hand because the people of the nation know that he must have the sword if he is to curb lawless and evil men. The presence of the policeman on the streets of a city represents the will of society to rise from the anarchy of might makes right to an ordered world in which force can be used in the interests of righteousness. Of course, the police power is often abused. The control of the police may be the means whereby those who hold special privileges seek to remain in power. But the conviction of mankind is that the abuses that go with the use of the police power are far less dangerous to society than the conditions that would immediately arise if the police power were abolished. And the policeman is rendered effective in the accomplishment of his task not by disarming him but by giving him power that is so adequate that it will never be seriously challenged by the lawless elements of the community.

If we could conceive of a world that was so organized that force among nations was used only by an international police force to support the decisions of a world court, we would draw near to Paul's conception of the proper use of force in international life. The fear of war between the forty-eight states of the United States of North America has to a large extent been abolished. The states are united in a union which establishes over them a national government. If disagreements between the states arise, the differences can be settled in courts of justice. Within the national government, there is power sufficient to enforce these decisions. Of course, there is danger that the more powerful states will so control the national government that the decisions of its courts may be unfair to the smaller states. But the injustice that may be done through such decisions is small compared to the injustice that would be done if every state had the right to take the law into its own hands and to use the appeal to might to settle its disputes in its own interests. In an interdependent world, we cannot permanently get away from the conception of a league of nations which has the power to use an international police force to enforce its decisions against an aggressor nation.

In Paul's world, there was in Rome a power that ruled the nations. The Romans were not idealists. They ruled at times with ruthless power. But in spite of all the criticisms we can make of the Romans, we must realize that they were the bearers to the world of the Roman law. They gave the ancient world a stable society and an ordered government. They made way externally for the proclamation of the gospel. Roman rule was much better than the chaos the world had known before the rise of Rome.

We must be realists in the modern world. We may dream of a world in which "the war drum throbs no longer and the battle-flags are furled in the Parliament of man, the Federation of the world." We may believe that some day the people of the world will call into being a society of nations in which nations can settle their differences without war. But we do not live in such a world. We must acknowledge that the system of collective security for our world has broken down.

In the international anarchy of our world, we cannot deny to any nation the right to use force to protect its citizens from international brigandage. We cannot place the sword in the hands of the magistrate to curb evil within the nation and at the same time deny to the state the right to use force to prevent the enslavement of the people to a ruthless foreign power. And if individuals may place the sword in the hands of the magistrate in order that a society may be created in which force if used at all is used in the interests of righteousness, we cannot deny to the nations the right to unite together to create an international force through which law and order can be established in international life.

No one can overestimate the folly and the futility of modern war. It is deeply tragic to see great empires using the labor of mankind to create the weapons with which men will destroy each other. The increased productive power that science has given to man should be used to raise the standard of living for all men. And modern war is more than a war of men. It is a war of propaganda. When nations fight, truth is always the first casualty. Gandhi has shown us that in some cases a policy of passive resistance is a means of protesting against tyranny which is far more effective than the appeal to arms. And the appeal to passive resistance is usually far less destructive of spiritual values.

But when all of the arguments against war as an instrument of national policy have been canvassed, we must realize that the world in which we live today is not a world in which a great state can function without the use of force. Paul was nothing if not a realist. And no realist can face our world and believe that the time has come for the nations that retain a sense of law and order and a concern for righteousness to disarm.

Has the United States the right to use the sword? It is very important that the sword in the hands of the United States should be used in the service of righteousness. The more powerful the nation the more important it is that those who direct her armed forces should be controlled by a high sense of responsibility to God and to man. And no one can deny that the "have" nations of the earth have contributed to the dilemma of the world in the beginning of 1941. The white race has no right permanently to fence off the undeveloped portions of the globe. The world will never be at peace until there is a free and fair movement of trade from one part of the world to another. A comparatively free movement of the world's population in response to economic opportunity is an essential feature of an enduring world order. But no sense of penitence for failures in the past can free a nation from the responsibility of facing in a realistic manner the world that actually exists today. A government that left the United States of America unprepared and therefore an easy prey to foreign invasion would be a government that betrayed the best interests of the nation. There are nations today that face the choice between war and a submission to a tyranny that is worse than the evils of war. In a sinful world, men do not face the choice between alternatives in which the devil is on one side and God and the angels are on the other. In our choice of alternatives, neither one may be all black or all white. Both may be grey. But one alternative may be a much darker grey than the other.

In times of anarchy, individuals must band together to create a government in which force can be used in the interests of righteousness. And the chaos of international life will never be overcome until the peoples of the earth who love righteousness and hate iniquity band themselves together to create a society of nations that shall again give security and order to our world. As one of the powerful nations of the earth, the United States of America cannot avoid her responsibility in this direction. Paul places the sword in the hands of the magistrate to curb evil and to establish justice. Would he not also recognize the sword in the hand of a nation if that sword is used to curb the lawless and irresponsible use of power by the other nations of the earth?

This does not mean that Paul would approve of all wars or even of most wars. Here as in other cases the Christian must decide in the light of the concrete situation that is faced by his nation. Most of us would like to avoid the agony of a decision such as this. But those who face alternatives in the midst of a sinful world cannot avoid the necessity for historical decision. The will of God for the Christian is not a rule that is general and universal. The will of God must come to us as an understanding of that which God would have us do in the midst of the possibilities of the situation we are actually facing.

Paul places the sword in the hands of the magistrate. The civil power must at times use the sword. The state cannot maintain order within the nation and defend the people of the nation from aggression by foreign powers without the use of the sword. But while Paul places the sword in the hands of the magistrate, he does not place it in the hands of the church. Paul gives to the Christian society only spiritual weapons for the defense and propagation of the gospel. In the opening verses of the thirteenth chapter of Romans, Paul gives the sword to the state. In the twelfth chapter, in the verses that immediately precede his discussion of the state, Paul writes to the Christian society in Rome, "Bless them that persecute you; bless, and curse not. . . . Render to no man evil for evil. Take thought for things honorable in the sight of all men. If it be possible, as much as in you lieth, be at peace with all men. Avenge not yourselves, beloved, but give place unto the wrath of God: for it is written, Vengeance belongeth unto me; I will recompense, saith the Lord. But if thine enemy hunger, feed him; if he thirst, give him to drink: for in so doing thou shalt heap coals of fire upon his head. Be not overcome of evil, but overcome evil with good." [14]

In these verses, Paul lays down for Christians a position very similar to that which Jesus gave in the Sermon on the Mount.[15] And Paul's statement in successive paragraphs of his position for the Christian society and his position for the state shows that in his mind there was no essential contradiction between the two. Paul tells the Christians to overcome evil with good. The Christians in the Roman Empire did not attempt to avenge themselves for the wrongs that were inflicted upon them. They met hatred with love. They were obedient to the laws of the Empire until they were ordered to worship the emperor. But the Christians consistently refused to deny their Lord. They met the power of Rome with passive disobedience. Even when the Empire sought to exterminate them, they never took the sword to defend themselves. They met the might of the

---

[14] Romans 12:14, 17-21.
[15] Matthew 5:38-48.

Empire with only spiritual force. The state may use the sword, but the Christian society within the state may not take the sword either for defense or for the propagation of the gospel.

There are many lands today in which the church is again facing persecution. Men are called upon again to bear witness to their faith through suffering or through death. And in this situation the Christian society must reveal again its capacity to resist with spiritual weapons the power of the state.

As we have followed the thought of Paul, we have thought with him of the state as existing in theory for beneficial ends. We have thought of the state as concerned to promote good and to restrain evil. In actual fact, a very different element all too often enters the life of the state. The state may become the instrument of tyranny and oppression. The ruler of the state may use his power in a way that is irresponsible and sinful. Evil men may gain control of the political order. They may seek to use the power of the state to enslave and exploit the people. Corrupt politicians may enrich themselves at the public expense.

The church faces a double task here. Her first and her most obvious duty is to remind the rulers of the nation that they are responsible to God for the way in which they use their power. Paul told all masters that they were to remember that they had a Master in heaven.[16] And it is in perfect harmony with the thought of Paul when we say that he would remind all rulers

---

[16] Ephesians 6:9; Colossians 4:1.

that they are not given an irresponsible use of power. In a democracy those who control power are responsible to the people. In a dictatorship this responsibility is to some extent avoided. But Paul would remind all rulers regardless of the form of government under which they operate that their first responsibility in the use of their power is to God. We must return to some conception such as this if we are ever to find a moral basis for international life. Christians should seek to place in positions of power men who will use their power with a high sense of responsibility to a righteous God.

One of the great tasks of prophecy in Israel was that of reminding the ruler of his responsibility to Jehovah. Some of the great scenes of Israel's history pass before us as we think of the prophets in their discharge of this responsibility. Samuel confronts Saul. Nathan condemns David. Elijah meets Ahab in Naboth's vineyard. Isaiah stands in the way of Ahaz, etc. Are we not justified in saying that one of the supreme tasks of the church is to hold steadily before every ruler the realization that his power is a God-given trust and that in his use of that power he is responsible to the God who has revealed Himself in Jesus Christ? The church does not build the political order. But she must build the men who build this order.

The breakdown of national and international life is at bottom a moral breakdown. No man and no nation can be permanently trusted with irresponsible power. The rulers of the nations must be made to realize that they are under a righteous God to whom they are responsible for their every act. Paul is abundantly aware that no man and no nation can permanently oppose the moral order. He knows that behind the moral order there is a righteous God who has said, "Vengeance belongeth unto me; I will recompense." Those who seek to break the moral order will ultimately break themselves upon it. God is not mocked. Men do not violate His laws with impunity. But Paul would also know that the permanent basis of any international society must lie in the recognition of the moral order by the rulers of the nations. When the rulers of all the nations have acknowledged a moral order that grounds in God, they will have laid the basis of an enduring league of nations. It must be the task of the church to lead men to acknowledge God in Christ as the Lord of their lives. It must be the task of Christians to place in positions of leadership and power those who will use that power with a sense of responsibility to a righteous God. And the church within the nation must assume the high function of reminding the rulers at all times that they must serve God.

In the second place, if the corruption of government remains permanently unchecked, Christians may be forced to raise the question as to whether the government that is in the seat of power can continue to be recognized as the power that is ordained of God. We face here one of those definite historical decisions with which the church is constantly confronted. Government is never perfect. The good government is never free from some corruption, and the bad government usually retains some of the characteristics of the just state. In a true democracy, there rests with the people the power to correct abuses in government by orderly processes. In most cases, Christians should endure injustice patiently until redress can be made within the framework of government. The injustice that is done through government is usually far less serious than the injustice that will come in a period of violent revolution.

But there may come times in the history of nations when the people of the nation are forced to recognize the fact that their government has become the total dissolution of the just state. If such a situation does arise, Christian citizens may be released from their sense of obligation to obey this government as ordained of God. And Christian citizens may face a historical situation in which they are called upon to associate themselves together in order that over against the false state there may be established a state which exists to reward the good and punish the evil.

Christianity is not identified with any one form of the economic order. And in a similar manner, Christianity is not identified with any one form of the political order. The church grew in the midst of the Roman Empire. She existed in the midst of the absolute monarchies of the Europe of the Middle Ages. The church has continued to grow within the democracies of England and North America. The church in China might enter into a day of opportunity in the midst of a dictatorship such as that of Chiang Kai-shek. Some forms of government are more congenial to the life of the church than others. But the church can live in the midst of any political order which carries the sword to "reward the good, and punish the evil, to rescue the poor and oppressed, and to make room externally for the free proclamation of the Gospel." [17]

But upon the church at times there must fall the responsibility of branding a definite form of government as the dissolution of the just state. It is in this vein that Karl Barth can write, "The office of the state which in Holy Scripture is set over against and alongside that of the Church, is fundamentally and absolutely denied and disowned in the deeds of National Socialism. According to the Scripture the office of the state is that of the servant of God who does not carry the sword to no purpose, but for the rewarding the good and punishing the evil, for the rescue of the poor and oppressed, and to make room externally for the free proclamation of the Gospel. And National Socialism in its deeds has fundamentally and absolutely denied and disowned this office. As a political experiment it has been revealed as a supreme destruction of all order, all justice and all freedom, and of all authority as well. . . . This state exists in and as the dissolution of the just State; this State is anarchy tempered by tyranny, or tyranny tempered by anarchy, but it is certainly *no* State. Or it is still a State, just in so far as, in some remaining parts, it is *not yet* National Socialist.

"The Church has a charge—according to her own conviction and in the application of her own confession —in the face of even one of the above mentioned facts, of saying with all definiteness of this thing that it is evil.

[17] From: *The Church and the Political Problem of Our Day*, by Karl Barth, page 52. By permission of Charles Scribner's Sons, publishers.

And this without an emotional appeal to moral standards, without wanting to sound the trump of Doom, but with the same objectivity with which she will give the name evil and not good to alcoholism, prostitution, gambling hells, and the like." [18]

In a similar way, we may face the judgment passed upon another political order by a missionary in China. This missionary writes, "We are representatives of the Prince of Peace, and exponents of the Gospel of Love, and yet we now find ourselves 100 per cent in support of the U. S. guns in the Pacific. Why? Because we know that unless something checks the power of darkness descending upon us, that these forces have resolved to exterminate the Church and uproot the organized teaching and preaching of Christ as we have it today." [19]

The quotations which we have given lead us inevitably to a consideration of a final problem, the problem of the freedom of the church in the midst of the political order. We have already touched upon this problem in our chapter on the church in the social struggle. But it now becomes necessary to look at this problem as, through the political order, pressure is exerted upon the church to throttle her witness. In the beginning of his ministry Paul asked merely to be let alone. The church he was founding had not come into any essential conflict with the Empire. When his letter to the Romans was written, Paul was able to think of the Roman power

---

[18] From: *The Church and the Political Problem of Our Day*, by Karl Barth, pages 52, 55, 56. By permission of Charles Scribner's Sons, publishers.

[19] For obvious reasons, the source of this quotation is not given.

as friendly to him. And during the whole of his first imprisonment, Paul was treated kindly by the Roman officials. While waiting for trial in Rome, he was permitted to have his own hired house.[20] And the Roman soldiers did not stop Paul from making his home the center of missionary activity in Rome.[21] In fact, he probably enjoyed from his guards a protection he would not otherwise have known. The epistles of the first imprisonment reflect this situation. Consider from this point of view Ephesians, Colossians, Philippians, and Philemon.

But with the growth of Christianity, a great change came over the attitude of the Roman state to the Christian society. This change took place during the life of Paul. Read from this point of view II Timothy and contrast this epistle with the earlier prison epistles. In II Timothy, Paul is a condemned man who is facing death. It is dangerous for others to acknowledge Paul as a friend. Demas has forsaken him. Only Luke is with him.[22] And Paul is filled with fears for Timothy his son in the faith.[23]

The change that is reflected in II Timothy is reflected much more clearly in the book of Revelation. In this book the state has become a church. Emperor worship has been used to test the Christian's loyalty to Christ. Rome has become Babylon, the great enemy of God's people. The church has entered a life and death struggle with the Empire.

---

[20] Acts 28:30.
[21] Acts 28:31.
[22] II Timothy 4:9-11.
[23] Consider in this connection II Timothy 2:1-13.

We are not to think that the struggle between the church that Paul founded and the Roman state was an accident. Evil men such as Nero might seek to turn the prejudice against the Christians to their own advantage. But some of the most terrible persecutions which the Christians faced came from Roman statesmen who thought they were persecuting the Christians for the good of the Empire. The ultimate question here was a question of loyalties. In the growing Christian society the Roman officials recognized that they faced a society within a society, an empire within an empire. And they recognized that the Christian society operated on a set of principles that were foreign to the life of Rome. They knew, too, that the Christian's loyalty to Jesus Christ came ahead of his loyalty to the Empire.

Rome did not object to religious tolerance. There was a place in the Roman pantheon for every kind of god. The conquered peoples of the Roman Empire were permitted to keep their own gods. But the Romans instinctively felt that in Christianity they had met with a different kind of force. The Christians refused to permit Jesus to be placed within the pantheon. They insisted that Jesus Christ was the *one Mediator* between God and man and that all the gods of the heathen were false gods, idols, creations of the minds of men.

Rome had met the Absolute, the Absolute as it appears in history. The true Absolute is the deadly enemy of all the false absolutes which men worship. The God-man destroys all of the man-gods. The Christian society exists as a conservative force within the life of the state. *But the Christian society is the one society that is able*

*to brand as idolatry the attempt of the state to deify it-
self.* The Christian society cannot live at peace with any
state which seeks to exalt itself into an object of religious worship.

The attempt of the state to control the witness of the
church may move along one of two lines or along both
lines at the same time. The state may attempt to control
the witness of the church until the voice of the church
is brought into harmony with the voice of the dominating culture that speaks through the state. The state will
always prefer to do this. Few rulers care to brand themselves as an anti-Christ charged with the extermination
of Christianity. But if the church resists the attempt
of the state to throttle its witness, then the power of
the state may be used in the effort to exterminate the
church.

Along with the attempt to control the witness of the
church, there usually goes the attempt to use the power
of the state to persecute or to exterminate the Christians
who will not yield to the "new understanding" of
Christianity. The true attitude of a Christian society as
it faces such a situation is expressed for us by Karl
Barth. He writes, "I maintain that the Evangelical
Church ought rather to elect to be thinned down till it
be a tiny group and go into the catacombs than make a
compact, even covertly, with this doctrine." [24]

The Christian faith cannot be identified with Japan's
vision for a new order in Asia. The Christian churches
both in China and in Japan must be free to be under

---

[24] From: *Theological Existence Today,* by Karl Barth, page 50. Hodder
& Stoughton, London. Used by permission.

Christ. No Christian should object to the attempt to purge the Christian message from many things that may have been read into it by the Western world. Perhaps the men of the East can see more clearly than the men of the West the way in which the white man has identified Western culture with the Christian message. Perhaps in India and China, and in Japan, Christians may arise who will understand more clearly than the men of America the meaning of the word of God spoken in Christ. Christianity began as an Oriental religion and the men of the East may come to understand more clearly than the men of the West the message of the Christian faith.

But it is one thing to say that the men of the East may understand Jesus Christ better than the men of the West. And it is a very different thing to say that the message of Christianity can be derived from the culture of the land in which it moves. Christianity can never permit any state to throttle the Christian message, to purge it of its universal elements, and to make it the bearer of a national culture that is not in harmony with the word of God in Christ. The battle line here is clear, and on this point the church cannot yield without disloyalty to her Lord.

CHAPTER XI

The Ecclesiastical Order=
The Ecumenical Church

+ +

THE man who hears and believes the word of God that is spoken in Jesus Christ always finds that he is confronted at once by an ecclesiastical order. The word which he believes has not come to him in a vacuum. In all probability, this word has come to him through a particular church, a church that is a member of one of the various denominations that are working in his community. When the believer wishes to make public confession of his faith and receive baptism, he finds that he cannot be baptized into the church universal without at the same time becoming a member of a local church, and a member of one of the various denominations into which the Christian church is at present divided.

As the believer becomes intimately associated with the ecclesiastical organizations which function in his world, he is certain to feel a sense of tension between the church that should exist and the church that actually does exist. If the believer becomes a student of the Bible and through his study enters into an understanding of Paul's conception of the church, he is certain to feel the chasm between the ecclesiastical order that confronts him and the Christian society that is envisioned in the New Testament. As he sees the existing ecclesiastical order against the background of the church of the New Testament, the Christian may find it more difficult to live in peace with the ecclesiastical order than to live as a Christian in the midst of the economic order or the political order.

The visible church exists in the midst of the world in various degrees of purity, of faith, and of life. Those who understand the depths of corruption to which the church may fall can also understand that at times the individual Christian may find it very difficult to realize a Christian life within the ecclesiastical order which dominates his world.

The concern of the Christian with the existing ecclesiastical order will go deeper than his realization of the inconsistencies that mark the lives of Christians. Judged from this point of view the New Testament church was not a perfect church. Paul's letters reveal to us a church that was marked at times by factions,[1] by heresies,[2] and by immoral living that was condoned by the Christian society.[3] The sins of Christians always injure the power of the influence of the church. But the church is a fellowship of pardoned sinners, and the power of sin, while broken, is not completely destroyed in the life of any Christian who continues to live in the midst of our sinful world.

The Christian may find that the leaders of the ecclesiastical organizations are corrupt. He may be forced to listen to appeals to sacrifice from men who draw large

---

[1] I Corinthians 1:10-12.
[2] Colossians 2:8—3:4.
[3] I Corinthians 5.

salaries and live comfortable and complacent lives while they call the Christian constituency to a sacrifice which they themselves are not willing to make. Like the Pharisees of old, the leaders of organized religion may be binding heavy burdens and grievous to be borne, and laying them on men's shoulders while they themselves will not move them with their finger. And at some periods in the history of the church the men at the head of the ecclesiastical machinery have sunk to the lowest depths of immorality and dishonesty.

The Christian may find that the church which confronts him is not loyal to the faith that was once for all delivered to the saints. The preaching that goes on in many churches may have very little relation to the redemptive word that was spoken in Jesus Christ.

The Christian may grasp with enthusiasm Paul's conception of a church in which all of the divisions of society are transcended. But when he turns from this vision to find its realization in the church in his community he may be sorely disappointed. He may find a church that has acquiesced in racial exclusiveness, in class prejudice, and in national arrogance. He may face a church that seems to be the puppet of class, or race, or nation.

Strangest of all of the developments of the church in the modern world to Paul would be the way in which the unity of the church is shattered by denominational divisions. He would find himself perplexed by the threefold cleavage by which the Christian world is divided into Roman Catholics, into the Greek Orthodox communion, and into the Protestant group. Even

more perplexing would be the way in which the Protestant world has been shivered into competing denominational bodies. Few things could seem more senseless
than the way in which Christians in old and settled
communities burden themselves and curtail their missionary giving to maintain two or three churches where
one church would be abundantly adequate for the
needs of the community. The believer who has caught
Paul's conception of the one church must find himself
in tension with the whole denominational system
through which organized religion operates in the
United States of America today.

Those who know intimately the whole life of the
church may find even deeper causes than those we have
mentioned for concern about the character of the existing ecclesiastical order. When Jesus came to earth he
found his bitterest opposition among the Pharisees, the
religious leaders of his time, and among the chief
priests, the men who administered the whole sacrificial
system of Judaism. And Jesus himself has said that it is
not possible for a prophet to perish outside of Jerusalem.[4] The prophet always finds his most deadly opposition in the centers of religious orthodoxy.

In *The Brothers Karamazov,* Dostoyevsky draws for
us his famous picture of the Grand Inquisitor. He sup-
poses that Jesus has returned to earth and has appeared
in Spain at Seville in the midst of the burning of the
heretics. Jesus is recognized by the people and also by
the old cardinal who is the grand inquisitor for the

---

[4] Luke 13:33.

church. The inquisitor orders Jesus arrested at once and placed in prison. At night the old man comes to the cell and explains to Jesus why the church which was founded in His name has been unable to follow His way of life. He closes his speech with the terrible words, "I shall burn Thee for coming to hinder us. For if anyone has ever deserved our fires, it is Thou. Tomorrow I shall burn Thee. Dixi." [5]

We naturally revolt against this scene, but we must feel an element of truth in it. If one had appeared in the life of the Spain of the inquisition and had fearlessly manifested in that world the attitudes of God, he would probably have been burned at the stake. And we cannot be too sure of what would happen to Jesus Christ if without any external authentication he would appear in our world. What would happen to him if he came veiled in the flesh and lived in American society a life in which he manifested attitudes of God? Would he be received by the church which bears his name? Would he fit into the ecclesiastical order of our day any better than he fitted into the ecclesiastical order of Judaism?

What would happen to Paul if he should appear on earth and seek to live in the Christian society of the twentieth century? What church would he join? What would he have to say about our denominational divisions? Could he be at home in class churches? Would he acquiesce in our racial exclusiveness? Would the Christian society honor him as a prophet or expel him as a heretic? Where would Paul find his intensest op-

---

[5] From: *The Brothers Karamazov*, by Dostoyevsky, page 270. By permission of Random House, Inc., publishers.

position? Would it be among those who are indifferent to religion? Or would it be in the centers of religious orthodoxy? Could the liberals stand Paul's message? Would the fundamentalists brand him as apostate?

All of these questions tend to bring out the chasm between the Christian society which actually exists today and the world fellowship in Christ which Paul envisioned. Those who are outside of the church are aware of this chasm. It is popular to praise Christ but to condemn the church which bears His name. It is popular to pour scorn on organized religion. There are some who feel that they must break with the existing ecclesiastical order if they are to be loyal to Christ. There are some who believe that the future of Christianity may lie with a remnant who are still loyal to Christ.

We have sought for the word of Paul to the Christian as he moves in the midst of the orders of society. We have faced Paul's word to the Christian who must live in the economic order or in the social order. What would Paul's word be to the Christian who must live in the midst of an ecclesiastical order that is still in many ways unchristian? Paul does not deal with the question directly because this question did not exist for him or for his converts. But on the basis of our knowledge of the whole thought of Paul we can suggest his answer. Paul's first word to the individual Christian in the midst of the economic order was to tolerate the existing economic order and to seek within the framework of that order to realize a Christian life. We can be sure he would speak a similar word to the individual Christian who faces the ecclesiastical order of our day.

We can be sure that Paul would tell each Christian to accept the ecclesiastical order which confronts him and to seek within that order to live a Christian life. This is the only course that is possible to the individual Christian. The Christian cannot wait until the evils of the ecclesiastical order are remedied. He must live his life with Christ now. And the Christian life cannot be lived in a vacuum. The Christian life must be lived against the background of the Christian society. This society will be found in an imperfect form within the churches. But it will be found within the churches and not outside of the churches. The presence of corruption in the church does not make it impossible for Jesus Christ to be found within the life of His church. The ecclesiastical life of Israel seldom reached greater depths of corruption than when the degenerate sons of Eli, Hophni and Phineas, administered the worship of the tabernacle at Shiloh. But when Hannah brought to the sanctuary a pure heart and an earnest prayer she was able to realize there the presence of her God.

The dark picture that we have drawn of the ecclesiastical order can be substantiated in all of its details, but it is not the whole picture, and it is not a true picture because it ignores the other side of the life of the church. Men who are outside of the church may be conscious of the chasm between the church as she ought to be and the church as she is. But those who stand at the heart of the life of the visible church are far more keenly conscious of her failures than those who stand outside and criticize. There may be hypocrites within the membership of the church, but there are many within the church who are not hypocrites. Corruption may exist among the leaders of the church, but within the leadership of the church there are to be found men of God who are living lives of fellowship with Jesus Christ. And the light of true faith has always continued to burn in the church in spite of the corruption of some of the leaders. Did not Jehovah find in the heart of Samuel a place to begin again when Eli and his sons had proved disloyal? The church may at times be the puppet of race or class or nation. But even when the church has acquiesced in racial injustice, a conscience will be found in the fellowship of the church which is not found in the world outside of the church. Class snobbery may be carried into the fellowship of the church. But within the church, class distinctions are always in struggle with the Pauline principle of a God with whom there is no respect of persons. The church may be hopelessly divided into denominational groups but the unity of the Christian world is expressing itself in spite of the denominational barriers to Christian fellowship. The church which has been branded as the puppet of the nation may prove to be the only society within the nation which dares to resist the attempt of the nation to deify itself.

Jesus sets for us an example in this respect. He was born in the midst of an ecclesiastical order which represented in many ways a denial of the will of God for the religious life of man. But we are told that it was His custom to go regularly to the synagogue at Nazareth. We know enough about Nazareth to know that the people of this synagogue were permeated by Jewish racial exclusiveness. In later years, they attempted to kill Jesus for suggesting that the word which they rejected might be given to the Gentiles.[6] We can imagine that there was very much in the synagogue that was almost intolerable to the boy of Nazareth who understood the will of God for man as no one else had ever understood it. But Jesus sought to serve God within the ecclesiastical order of His day. At twelve, He went for the first time to the temple. The temple was at the time the center of much of the corruption of Jewish ecclesiastical life. In later years, Jesus called the place a den of thieves. But the temple remained to Jesus His Father's house and a place of prayer.

The Christian will best serve God as he accepts the ecclesiastical order of his day and seeks within it to do the will of God. But the Christian should not accept the ecclesiastical order without a sense of tension with it. In saying that the Christian should tolerate the ecclesiastical order and seek within it to serve God, we do not mean that the Christian should permanently acquiesce in the imperfections of the existing ecclesiastical order. Basic to the whole thought of the Reformation there is the conception that the existing church in every age should be purified by the comparison of this church with the church that is envisioned in the New Testament. In this way, the Apostle Paul can become a great dynamic force in the purging of the existing ecclesiastical order in our world. The church in every age must

---

[6] Luke 4:16-30.

be weighed in the balance against the vision of the church that is set forth in the letters of Paul.

The classic example of this process in history is found in the experience of the great Reformers. Calvin and Luther found themselves in the midst of an ecclesiastical order which had sunk to inconceivable depths of corruption. The Communion service which Paul described had been transformed into the idolatry of the Mass. The sale of indulgences had become a scandal in Christendom. The individual priesthood of believers which Paul proclaimed had been destroyed by the doctrine that the priest had the power on earth to forgive sins. The simple church organization which Paul had set up had been developed into a hierarchy centering in the college of cardinals and the infallible Pope. The adoration of Mary and the use in worship of the images of the saints had introduced into the church a subtle form of idolatry.

The Reformers faced a highly developed system in which through the centuries accretions had been made to the original content of the gospel message. They knew that they faced a corrupt system, an ecclesiastical order which had departed from the will of God for His church. But the problem before them was how to purify this system without completely destroying an order which contained much of good as well as much of evil. The principle which the Reformers adopted as the basis of their attempt to reform the life of the church is what is known as the Scriptural principle. They insisted that the existing ecclesiastical organization must be purified by being brought into harmony with the vision of the church that is found in the New Testament. This principle was expressed in its strongest form in the determination to permit in the life of the church nothing which was not commanded in the New Testament. It was expressed in a milder form in the determination to remove from the life of the church everything that was forbidden in the New Testament. The Reform movement held roughly to the principle in its strongest form. The Lutherans adopted the milder form of the principle and retained many things which Calvin cast out. Within the Protestant world as a whole the practice of the church alternated between the two forms in which the principle was stated. But within the whole Protestant Reformation the Scriptural principle was recognized. As Karl Barth says, "At their very beginnings the Reformed churches saw that truth is contained only in the word of God, that the word of God for them lay only in the Old and New Testaments, and that every doctrine must therefore be measured against an unchangeable and impassible standard discoverable in the Scriptures. What one may be moved to say concerning God, the world, and man because he *must* say it, having let the Scriptures speak to him— the Scriptures themselves, and not the Scriptures interpreted by any particular tradition; the whole Scriptures, and not a part of them chosen to suit a preconceived theory; the Scriptures and not the utterances of pious men of the past or present which might be confused with them; the Scriptures, and not without the significant word of the Spirit which sustains them—what, after those Scriptures have spoken to him, one may be moved to say in fear and trembling concerning the things about which man may of himself say nothing, or only foolishness, that, if we may judge from our beginnings, is Reformed doctrine." [7]

On the basis of the Scriptural principle, the Reformers set out to reform a corrupt ecclesiastical order. They based their message on the *whole Bible* but they found the *bulk* of their material for the reformation of the church in the writings of Paul. Paul spoke through Luther and Calvin as those men sought to reform the message of the church. Paul's doctrine of justification by faith alone was rediscovered and through it the power of the whole Roman system was broken. Paul's conception of the one Mediator between God and man, the man Christ Jesus, was set against the whole system of mediation through priests, or angels, or saints, or the virgin Mary. Calvin reproduced in France the organization of the persecuted church of the New Testament. Over against the hierarchy of Rome, he built a church that was governed by elders and deacons elected by the people. He studied the government of the church in the New Testament, and from it he laid the foundations of the Presbyterian system of church government. He created in history a democratic system in which the church was governed by representatives elected by the people and responsible to the people.

Our interest at present is not in the details of the reformation that was carried out under Calvin and Luther but in the principle upon which this reforma-

---

[7] From: *The Word of God and the Word of Man*, by Karl Barth, page 241. Copyright, The Pilgrim Press. Used by permission.

tion proceeded. It was a reformation that was in harmony with the inner sources of the life of the church. The church was not reformed by the application of some principle that was foreign to her origin. The church was reformed by a return to the vision of the church that was found in Paul. The church went backward to the sources of her life before she was able to go forward to her task in the world.

The Protestant churches go back to the Reformation. The Presbyterian church, for example, goes back to John Knox and to John Calvin and through them to Martin Luther. But no one could claim that in their faith and life the Protestant churches of the modern world are identified with the persecuted church of France which Calvin founded or with the persecuted church of the New Testament which Calvin adopted as his model. The principle which Calvin adopted should be a purifying principle in the life of the church in every generation. The modern church needs to correct its message by the message which Paul proclaimed. The whole of the ecclesiastical order of our day needs to be called into question by the return of Christians to Paul's vision of the church and by the attempt of Christians to realize again in history a Christian society which will be in harmony with Paul's conception of the church as the body of Christ in the midst of the life of the world.

In a book called *The Christian Message for the World Today,* a book that was published in 1934 by a number of Christian leaders in America, a significant statement is found. In the foreword of the book, these leaders express their common faith by saying, "We are agreed in holding that Christian missions look toward the creation of a world society permeated in every aspect of its life by the spirit of Jesus Christ; that society is to be one in which love prevails, *breaking down divisive barriers between nation and nation, race and race, class and class.* We hold no easy-going optimism about human progress; we are painfully aware that we can maintain this vision of the outcome only by a heroic venture of faith. But the Christian church, by reason of its very gospel, can do no less than witness to and work for such a society." [8]

The vision of a Christian society which these church leaders hold is in harmony with that vision of the Christian society which in the beginning of the life of the church the Apostle Paul set forth. The same vision of a Christian fellowship has been set forth in this book as the message of Paul to our world. But where can such a Christian society be found? If it is present in the existing ecclesiastical order it is found in germ only. The chasm between the church as she exists in history and the vision which Paul had for the church is clear to all of us. What is the task of the Christian in our generation in the light of the chasm between the church as she is and the church as she ought to be? The answer is that the Christian today must lay firm hold of Paul's understanding of the nature of the Christian society.

---

[8] From: *The Christian Message for the World Today,* page 8. By permission of The Round Table Press, Inc., publishers.

The Christian leaders responsible for the publication of this book are E. Stanley Jones, Kenneth Scott Latourette, John A. Mackay, Francis J. McConnell, Basil Mathews, Francis P. Miller, William Patton, Henry P. VanDusen, Luther Allan Weigle.

When he has done this, he must seek in the spirit of Calvin and Luther to challenge those things in the life of the church which are not in harmony with the insights into the nature of the Christian society which Paul has given us. The Christian must accept the existing ecclesiastical order. He must take his place in the life of the church which actually exists today. But the Christian must remain in permanent tension with everything in the existing ecclesiastical order which is out of harmony with the vision of the church which is found in the New Testament. This is the message of Paul to the Christian as he moves in the midst of the ecclesiastical order. If Paul is understood in this way, he may become a tremendous and dynamic force in the life of the church today. Paul has both a conservative and a radical message to the Christian in the midst of the orders of society. In the same sense, he has both a conservative and a radical message to the Christian in the midst of the ecclesiastical order. The voice which speaks through Paul to the church today is a voice that calls to Christians everywhere to re-examine the life of the church in the light of the vision of the church which is found in the New Testament. If this voice is heeded, Paul can become a transforming power in the midst of the ecclesiastical order today.

It would be superfluous for us to work through again in this chapter on the ecclesiastical order Paul's message to the church in the midst of the orders of society. We have already dealt with Paul's vision of the church as a society "breaking down divisive barriers between nation and nation, race and race, class and class." But

we should not close the chapter on the ecclesiastical
order without considering Paul's message concerning
the unity of the church. The existing ecclesiastical order
reveals a divided Christendom. In saying this we do not
refer to the obvious fact that the church is organized
along geographical lines. The church must always be
organized into local congregations. The church in the
United States would naturally function as one unit and
the church in Canada as another unit. We do refer to
the fact that the church of England confesses her faith
in such a way as to come at many points into irreconcilable conflict with the confession of faith that is found in
the church of Scotland. We do refer to the fact that the
Protestant and the Catholic communions go back to the
same New Testament for their message but confess
their faith in creeds which contradict each other. We do
refer to the fact that when Christians gather together in
world conferences they cannot gather at a common
Communion table. The existing ecclesiastical order is
divided into churches that stand over against each other.
They disagree fundamentally in their understanding of
the content of the "faith which was once for all delivered unto the saints." [9] The unity of Christendom is
shattered by the existence within Christendom of a
multiplicity of churches each of which comes forward
with its separate answer as to the meaning of the word
of God which was spoken in Jesus Christ.

Concerning the multiplicity of the churches, Karl
Barth writes, "In fact, we have no right to explain the

[9] Jude 3.

multiplicity of the churches at all. We have to deal with it as we deal with sin, our own and others, to recognize it as a fact, to understand it as the impossible thing which has intruded itself, as guilt which we must take upon ourselves, without the power to liberate ourselves from it. We must not allow ourselves to acquiesce in its reality; rather we must pray that it be forgiven and removed, and be ready to do whatever God's will and command may enjoin in respect of it.

"Or is there perhaps some other possible way than that of dealing with the multiplicity of the churches as we deal with sin, our own and others? If Christ is indeed, as we saw, the unity of the church, then the only multiplicity which can be normal is that *within* the Church, namely that of the local communities, of the gifts of the Spirit, of the believers of each sex, language, and race, and there can be no multiplicity of the churches. It is then unthinkable that to those multiplicities which are rooted in unity we should have to add that which tears it in pieces; unthinkable that great entire groups of communities should stand over against each other in such a way that their doctrines and confessions of faith are mutually contradictory; that what is called revelation in one place should be called error elsewhere, that what is here revered as dogma should there be regarded as heresy; that the ordinances of one group should be stigmatised by another as alien, unacceptable, or even intolerable: that the adherents of the one should be at one with those of another in every conceivable point except that they are unable to pray together, to preach and hear God's word together, and to join together in Holy Communion.

"It is unthinkable that whichever way one looks and listens, one should hear people saying in quiet or vehement tones, with kindly under-statement or in undisguised sternness, 'You have a different spirit from ours.' Yet that is just what actually results from the multiplicity of the churches; to wash our hands of it, or to prescribe doses of love, patience, and tolerance as a cure is futile. Such prescriptions may serve our turn almost anywhere else, but it is hopeless to mediate between churches by such methods—unless the churches are dead already. If they are alive, and if we are listening for Christ's voice, then it is not a matter of opinion but of faith that over against the doctrine, order, and life of other churches we should utter a more or less emphatic *No* at certain decision points, that we should draw the line and thus be compelled to endorse the multiplicity of the churches." [10]

Karl Barth states for us the reason that as Christians we can never permanently acquiesce in the multiplicity of the churches. There are many reasons which impel us to seek the lost unity of Christendom. In unity, there is strength. The church today is engaged in a life-and-death struggle with the powers of the world. A church that is hopelessly divided and at war with itself will be weak at a time when it is imperative that she should be strong. The church on the mission field is weak because she is divided. And in many lands the church at

[10] From: *The Church and the Churches,* by Karl Barth, pages 40, 42-44. By permission of W. B. Eerdmans Publishing Company.

home faces a rising anti-Christian movement which threatens her existence. But passing over these secondary reasons for our interest in church unity, Barth writes, "Yet it must be made clear at the outset that all these motives are merely secondary when compared with another authoritative impulse which forces this question upon us. I refer to that one and only imperative and obligatory task from which the Church derives its existence, a task which lies upon every man who, as a responsible being, has accepted the cause of the Church as his own. This task emerges immediately from the fact that the one and only Word of God has once for all been uttered, for all men to heed, in the fact of the Incarnation: in the man Christ Jesus, in whom the sin of all men, their contradiction against God and their own inner self-contradiction is done to death, taken away, forgiven, and exists no more. The task from which the Church derives its being is to proclaim that this has really happened and to summon men to believe in its reality. It has therefore no life of its own, but lives as the body of which the crucified and risen Christ is the Head; that is to say, it lives in and with this commission. The same thing is true of each individual who is a member of this body. It is this task and commission which fundamentally impels and compels us to ask after the unity of the Church.

"The task as thus committed contemplates no multiplicity of churches. The New Testament speaks of a variety of communities, of gifts, and of persons within the one Church. But this manifoldness has no independent significance. Its origin, its rights, and its limits are to be found in the unity, or rather in the One, in Jesus Christ as the one Son of God, the bestower of the one Holy Spirit." [11]

Barth has led us to the place at which we are prepared to hear the message which Paul would speak to a divided Christendom. He writes to the Ephesians, "I therefore, the prisoner in the Lord, beseech you to walk worthily of the calling wherewith ye were called . . . giving diligence to keep the unity of the Spirit in the bond of peace. There is one body, and one Spirit, even as also ye were called in one hope of your calling; one Lord, one faith, one baptism, one God and Father of all, who is over all, and through all, and in all." [12]

In the verses that follow immediately after this passage, Paul speaks of the diversity of gifts which we may expect within the one church. He writes, "But unto each one of us was the grace given according to the measure of the gift of Christ. . . . And he gave some to be apostles; and some, prophets; and some, evangelists; and some, pastors and teachers; for the perfecting of the saints, unto the work of ministering, unto the building up of the body of Christ: till we all attain unto the unity of the faith, etc." [13]

But in the thought of Paul the diversity of gifts is not to lead to a multiplicity of churches. These functions are to be exercised in the church in order that we may all come to the *unity* of the faith. And the unity of the

---

[11] From: *The Church and the Churches,* by Karl Barth, pages 22, 24. By permission of W. B. Eerdmans Publishing Company.

[12] Ephesians 4:1-6.

[13] Ephesians 4:7, 11-13a.

church is not a goal which man can achieve by his own efforts. The unity of the church is to be found in the God-given unity of the faith by which the church must live.

We would bring out the thought of verse 3 if we would paraphrase it, "striving earnestly to preserve your spiritual unity." The Christians are urged to hold on to the unity that they already have. This unity is defined in verses 4 and 5. "There is one body, and one Spirit, even as also you were called in one hope of your calling; one Lord, one faith, one baptism, one God and Father of all." We do not have to go into a detailed analysis of these verses in order to bring out their essential truth. Over against the multiplicity of the churches with their conflicting creeds there is set the unity of the Christian faith. There is only one Jesus Christ, there is only one Holy Spirit. There is only one God. There is only one faith. There is only one baptism. There is only one sacrament of the Lord's Supper. There is only one heaven. There is only one church.

Paul affirms the unity of the Christian faith. In doing this he proclaims that the multiplicity of the churches with their conflicting creeds is a condition which cannot permanently be tolerated within Christendom. The conflicting answers of the various churches as to the meaning of the one word that was spoken in Jesus Christ is evidence that in the creeds of the churches truth is mixed with error and that probably none of them have as yet attained unto God's truth. The churches must not settle themselves to rest comfortably and complacently in the presence of their conflicting answers as to the meaning of the word of God in Christ. It is sheer arrogance for a little section of Christendom to assume that its faith is THE CHRISTIAN FAITH and that all the rest of the Christian world is in error. The multiplicity of the churches should thrust the whole church into an *agony* of decision and into the determination that this sinful situation shall not be permanently characteristic of the Christian world. Paul would set in the heart of every Christian a divine unrest, an unrest that cannot be at rest until we all attain unto the *unity* of the faith.

All Christians would acknowledge the unity of the Christian faith. There is one Jesus Christ, one Holy Spirit, one God and Father of us all, one church, one faith, one baptism. No Christian can deny the great truth which Paul asserts. But the road to the realization of the unity of the faith is not an easy road. The unity of the Christian world will not be reached by a toleration which is unconcerned with doctrine. The churches cannot agree to co-operate in their active ministry while they disagree fundamentally in their basic thinking. Church union must not be culminated in indifference to truth. On this point Karl Barth strikes a true note when he says, "Let us not deceive ourselves. The union of the churches into the oneness of the Church would mean more than mutual tolerance, respect, and co-operation; more than readiness to hear and to understand each other; more than an emotional sense of oneness in the possession of some ineffable common link; more than that we, being one in faith, hope, and charity, could worship together in one accord. Above all it would mean, as the decisive test of unity, that we should join in making confession of our faith and thus should unitedly proclaim it to the world, and so fulfill that commandment of Jesus on which the Church is based. The message and witness, given by the Church's teaching, order, and life must utter one voice, however manifold in the diversity of languages, gifts, of place and persons. A union of the Churches in the sense of that task which is so seriously laid upon the Church would mean a union of the confessions into one unanimous Confession. If we remain on the level where the confessions are divided, we remain where the multiplicity of the churches is inevitable." [14]

The only form of church union which can be permanently helpful is the church union that is made possible because the churches entering into it have reached a common understanding of the meaning of the Christian faith. And Barth is right when he asserts, "The step away from a particular to a common confession must have no taint of compromise, or of an assent to forms and formulae of union which would camouflage division without transcending it. A church taking such a step must be known to act with perfect truthfulness and loyalty." [15]

The final realization of the unity of the faith will not come to pass through indifference to doctrine. It will come as the churches in their realization of the sin and

---

[14] From: *The Church and the Churches,* by Karl Barth, pages 66, 67. By permission of W. B. Eerdmans Publishing Company.

[15] From: *The Church and the Churches,* by Karl Barth, page 70. By permission of W. B. Eerdmans Publishing Company.

guilt they must bear because of the multiplicity of the churches go back to their origins and reject the foreign elements that have been engrafted into the thought and life of the church. As Christians in each church seek to rediscover the CHRISTIAN FAITH, they will work toward a common goal. And just in proportion as each church succeeds in recovering the lost unity of the FAITH, this church will be brought nearer to the place of union with other churches that have also laid hold of the ONE FAITH. The goal of church union must be the redis-covery by all Christians everywhere of the faith that was "once for all delivered unto the saints." [16]

We must not lose our vision of the goal, but at the same time we can mark some of the steps that may lead to this goal. The process of conversation between the churches must go on. Oxford and Edinburgh and Madras are movements in the right direction. Already the Church exists in the churches. Increasingly Chris-tians should seek to realize the essential unity that they already have. In many cases, the churches have already moved to a common faith which they continue to con-fess through conflicting symbols. We must go behind words and symbols to the basic convictions of the church. There is a large area of truth that is common to all of the Protestant creeds.

We must learn to distinguish between essentials and non-essentials. Christians might very properly be per-mitted to disagree on many things if the great essentials of the faith were held in common. We must rediscover

---

[16] Jude 3.

in Protestantism a new sense of the sin of schism. We have had in the Protestant world a strong sense of the sin of heresy. But Protestants as a whole do not feel keenly enough their sin in perpetuating needless divisions in the body of Christ. Those who needlessly perpetuate schism in the church may be guilty of a sin that at times is as heinous in the sight of God as the sin of heresy. As a step toward the larger unity of the church, we should work in the immediate future toward the reunion of those branches of the church which are most closely associated in faith and life. The reunion of the various Methodist bodies sets for Protestantism as a whole an example which should be a source of inspiration to those communities which have not yet achieved union within their own family of churches. In this respect, the reunion of the various Presbyterian and Reformed bodies in America should be a goal of Presbyterians everywhere. These churches possess a common doctrinal background and a common ecclesiastical organization. They should be able to achieve a unity of faith which would make their reunion flow from their confession of a common faith. Some generation of Presbyterians will achieve this union. They will achieve it because they have moved in obedience to Christ. And if we cannot realize the unity of the faith in the churches that are most closely associated with us in faith and order, what hope is there for the final overcoming of the multiplicity of the churches in the realization of the ONE CHURCH which gives expression to the ONE FAITH?

The task of the church in the ecclesiastical order is a

gigantic task. The church must move within the existing ecclesiastical order. She must seek to purify this order, by calling in question those things in the ecclesiastical order which do not conform to the vision of the church which is set forth in the New Testament. She must seek to recover the lost unity of the Christian faith. She must seek to realize in history a Christian society in which love prevails, a society which "breaks down divisive barriers between race and race, nation and nation, class and class." Who is sufficient for these things? We face a task which is lofty and arduous beyond measure, a task of superhuman magnitude.

As Barth says, "What voice or summons will be mighty enough to utter God's word in such tones to a church like the Roman, the Lutheran, or the Reformed, to these three together and all the others with them that they could respond with one confession and so return to the unity of the Church?" [17] What voice is mighty enough to speak to Christians in America, in Japan, in China, and in Germany, to Christians in the white race and to Christians in the colored races, to Christians in the upper classes of society, and to Christians in the bourgeois and to Christians in the proletariat, to Christians everywhere, in the demand that they shall realize the brotherhood of man in Christ, a brotherhood which transcends all of the divisions of our earthly life? Who is able to call into historical existence the church which Paul envisioned—the church which might save our world?

[17] From: *The Church and the Churches,* by Karl Barth, page 73. By permission of W. B. Eerdmans Publishing Company.

Paul had his vision of a Christian society and his prayer for its realization. To the Ephesians, he writes, "For this cause I bow my knees unto the Father, from whom every family in heaven and on earth is named, that he would grant you, according to the riches of his glory, that ye may be strengthened with power through his Spirit in the inward man; that Christ may dwell in your hearts through faith; to the end that ye, being rooted and grounded in love, may be strong to apprehend with all the saints what is the breadth and length and height and depth, and to know the love of Christ which passeth knowledge, that ye may be filled unto all the fulness of God." [18]

And having given expression to his vision for a Christian society, Paul turns to the ONLY ONE who is able to make this vision a reality. In the next sentence, he says, "Now unto him that is able to do exceeding abundantly above all that we ask or think, according to the power that worketh in us, unto him be the glory in the church and in Christ Jesus unto all generations for ever and ever. Amen." [19]

The Christ who is the power who is already at work in the churches is able to work through them to the establishing in history of THE CHURCH which He revealed to the world through His great apostle. The Christ who moved through Paul to the calling into being of the world church in the Roman Empire is able to move through His followers today to the reformation of the ecclesiastical order and to the realization in our world

---

[18] Ephesians 3:14-19.
[19] Ephesians 3:20, 21.

of THE CHRISTIAN SOCIETY. The divine voice which speaks through Paul would call us to this task today.

Paul stood in the presence of a divine command. Many years later he was able to say to King Agrippa, "I was not disobedient unto the heavenly vision." [20] The call to the church today is to visualize the Christian society that is set forth as her goal and to move toward the realization of this goal as she hears and obeys the command of her Lord. If she does this, she may know that she serves a Christ who is able to do exceeding abundantly above all that she may ask or think.

---

[20] Acts 26:19.

Index